DECEMBER BRIDE

Ireland Into Film

Series editors:
Keith Hopper (text) and Gráinne Humphreys (images)

Ireland into Film is the first project in a number of planned
collaborations between Cork University Press and the Film
Institute of Ireland. The general aim of this publishing initiative
is to increase the critical understanding of 'Irish' Film (i.e. films
made in, or about, Ireland). This particular series brings together
writers and scholars from the fields of Film and Literary Studies
to examine notable adaptations of Irish literary texts.

Other titles available in this series:

The Dead (Kevin Barry)
This Other Eden (Fidelma Farley)

Forthcoming titles:

The Informer (Patrick F. Sheeran)
The Field (Cheryl Herr)
Nora (Gerardine Meaney)
The Quiet Man (Luke Gibbons)
The Butcher Boy (Colin MacCabe)

Ireland Into Film

DECEMBER BRIDE

Lance Pettitt

CORK UNIVERSITY PRESS

in association with
THE FILM INSTITUTE OF IRELAND

First published in 2001 by
Cork University Press
Cork
Ireland

© Lance Pettitt 2001
Reprinted 2016

British Library Cataloguing in Publication Data
A CIP catalogue record for this book is available from the British Library.

ISBN 978 1 859 18290 1

Typesetting by Red Barn Publishing, Skeagh, Skibbereen

Printed and bound by CPI Group (UK) Ltd, Croydon, CR0 4YY

Ireland into Film receives financial assistance from
the Arts Council / An Chomhairle Ealaíon and the Film Institute of Ireland

This book is dedicated to all of those who have tested the taboo and been lucky and daring enough to find out that three is not always a crowd.

CONTENTS

List of Illustrations   viii

Acknowledgements   ix

Introduction   1

1   The Novel and its Contexts   9

2   Film Production Contexts   28

3   Movie Matters: Inter-Texts and Text   48

Conclusion: Offering a Future with Difference   73

Credits   77

Notes   81

Bibliography   89

LIST OF ILLUSTRATIONS

Plate 1.	Sam Hanna Bell	11
Plate 2.	Orange culture	14
Plate 3.	Front cover of *December Bride* (1982)	25
Plate 4.	Front cover of *December Bride* (1989)	26
Plate 5.	Independence isolated	37
Plate 6.	Thaddeus O'Sullivan	38
Plate 7.	Expressive framing and cinematography	39
Plate 8.	Thaddeus O'Sullivan directs Donal McCann and Saskia Reeves	43
Plate 9.	Cinema as art	46
Plate 10.	Light House Cinema publicity poster	51
Plate 11.	*Le Bonheur*	53
Plate 12.	Taboo triangular desires	56
Plate 13.	Son/lover, Mother/lover	57
Plate 14.	Who's your daddy?	61
Plate 15.	The good shepherd and his flock	62
Plate 16.	Defiant motherhood	65
Plate 17.	Taboo three-way desire	69

Acknowledgements

I would like to thank Thaddeus O'Sullivan, David Rudkin, Jonathan Cavendish and Little Bird Films for their co-operation in the research towards this book. Thaddeus in particular made a number of important documents, photographs and correspondence available and has given a great deal of time to let me interview him and follow up a myriad of other enquiries.

I am grateful to Keith Hopper for commissioning me to write for this new joint publishing venture, allowing me the luxury of choosing my own topic and keeping me going when things were tough. His conception for the series has opened up a new vista for research and debate that is to be warmly welcomed. Sara Wilbourne and the production team at Cork University Press have ensured that the book was carefully designed and efficiently produced. I would like to express my gratitude to Anne Tannahill and The Blackstaff Press for being so helpful in my research and for giving permission to reproduce the different front covers from the novel. Special thanks are due to Gráinne Humphreys for her sterling work on the visual material for the book and for supplying review materials from the archive at the Film Institute in Dublin. I would like to offer sincere thanks and best wishes for the future to my colleague and métier, Liam Harte. During a particularly testing semester, he read chapters 1 and 2 with his usual critical acuity and attention to detail, suggesting several important improvements. It has been a pleasure and privilege to work with him over the last decade and I want to record my appreciation for his dedicated professionalism, collegiate support and his personal friendship.

I would also like to thank: Emma Keogh at the Film Institute of Ireland, the BFI Stills Library, BFI Video, Carlton Television, Cine-Tamaris and Paladium Films for film stills permissions, the ITC Library in London, Belfast Public Library, Malachi Moran at the

RTÉ Reference Library, RTÉ Audience Research, Fergus Bell, Simon Mein, Fidelma Farley, Colin Crichton at the *Down Recorder*, *In Dublin* and St Mary's College Research Fund for financing a trip to Belfast. I warmly acknowledge the support of the Cultural Relations Committee, Department of Foreign Affairs, Dublin, that allowed me to deliver a paper on which chapter 3 is based. In the same vein, Rob Savage and Shane Murphy kindly invited me to deliver research papers, respectively, to the Irish Studies Programme, Boston College and the Institute of Irish and Scottish Studies at Aberdeen University. The discussions that followed were extremely useful but I remain, of course, entirely responsible for the finished product.

The editors would also like to thank Sheila Pratschke, Lar Joye, Michael Davitt, Luke Dodd, Ellen Hazelkorn, Dennis Kennedy, Kevin Rockett, Seán Ryder, St Cross College (Oxford), the School of Irish Studies Foundation and the Arts Council of Ireland. Special thanks to Seán Ryder.

INTRODUCTION

December Bride (1990) puts 'Ireland into film' in a provocative manner. It remains Thaddeus O'Sullivan's most accomplished film to date and this book examines it in order to understand better the processes that make for a satisfying adaptation from fiction to film. More broadly, this book seeks to challenge the traditional view of film adaptations being somehow 'secondary' to the original texts on which they are based. In approaching this task, we first need to acknowledge the fact that 'December Bride' takes *multiple* forms of existence as a cultural text: as the début novel by Sam Hanna Bell published in 1951, the David Rudkin screenplay written in 1988–89 (though this itself went through several drafts) and O'Sullivan's film which was shown in cinemas during 1990–91. This lineage might seem straightforward enough. However, it is less well known that Bell himself adapted his own novel into a stage script with the gruff-sounding title, *That Woman from Rathard*, produced by the Ulster Group Theatre, Belfast, in 1955, and wrote another version for radio for BBC Northern Ireland in 1963.[1] Another, unproduced, screen adaptation has been written by the novelist Maurice Leitch. Given these facts, we are bound to question the comforting notion of a definitive, singular, 'original text'.

To take this further, we only have to consider that 'December bride' as a common expression existed as part of wider, oral culture on which Bell drew for the novel's title. In Ulster-Scots dialect a 'December bride' refers somewhat pejoratively to a woman who marries late in life. Secondly, the narrative core of both novel and film – a *ménage à trois* between a woman and two brothers on a farm – came to Bell in the form of a Belfast pub 'story' told by a childhood friend. More than a lad's 'tall tale' told in drink, it was based on actual circumstances that were rather closer to home. Bell's biographer confirms that the maternal side of his family (the McIlveens) knew of such a scenario 'perhaps involving distant relations of their own'[2] in Raffery, County Down, where the author spent part of his childhood. So, the point established here is that, as well as having a complicated 'hard text' existence, in a very real sense 'December Bride' pre-existed the novel in oral forms within the popular culture and family history in which Bell grew up.

In the broader spirit of this series, the present study tries also to evaluate the centrifugal significance of a film adaptation – its 'after-life' beyond its existence as a cinema product. Within this cultural studies ambit, it then becomes of interest to trace its appearance on broadcast television and its release on home video in 1992.[3] This is part of a critical process – a decade on from its first screening at the Grand Cinema in Downpatrick, Northern Ireland, and its world première at the Dublin Film Festival on 22 February 1990 – of judging how *December Bride* may be located within a critical history of Irish cinema. To some readers, filmgoers and literary critics, it might seem perverse not to privilege Bell's novel as the pattern from which all other versions are cut, but this study does not see the novel as intrinsically 'better' than a screen version; indeed, it is argued that adaptations do not exist in a kind of necrophagous relation to originary novels. Rather, using *December Bride* as a test case, this book explores the idea that novel adaptations (in both senses of that phrase) invite and produce a kind of textual interdependency. This much was noted by the critic Robert Greacen, one of Bell's contemporaries who lived to see *December Bride* on a cinema screen. In an obituary he observed shrewdly that, 'now made into a memorable film, [it] will ensure a place for him [Bell] in the Irish fiction tradition for generations to come'.[4] Here, indeed, Greacen suggests that, although the novel may have had a 'local' interest, it was not read much outside of Ireland,[5] and that the effect of the film was to reinvigorate both critical and reading interest in Bell, thus making a space for him as a novelist of repute. We will examine Bell's qualities and standing as a writer of fiction more fully in Chapter 2, but it is enough to register here that films may inadvertently stimulate re-evaluations to take place in another critical field.[6]

The film of *December Bride* – like most other cultural artefacts – may be interpreted as being a product of its time; it comes out of a particular conjuncture of elements. This comprises the history of the social, political and cultural contexts in which the film was written, produced, exhibited and subsequently circulated. This conjuncture is shaped by the particular circumstances of the film's funding sources and the size of the budget, the conception of the adaptation, the style of writing and the directional choices. In addition, particular technical talent is brought to bear to execute the filming, acting performances and the production design. Finally, the marketing of the film, the circumstances of its release and its critical reception all contribute to its meaningfulness as a cinematic text.

Here I will briefly introduce the key social, political and cultural contexts of the late 1980s, the period in which O'Sullivan's film was conceived and produced. This decade has been characterized in social terms as one of conservative retrenchment both within Ireland and Britain, if not further afield as well. The typical indicators of this in relation to the Republic of Ireland are the after-effects of the Pope's visit to Dublin in 1979 and the major referenda of 1983 and 1986 that constitutionally reinforced the existing prohibitions on abortion and divorce. Whilst the Catholic Church and the state actually became more detached in Ireland over traditional social and moral questions during the 1980s, there was a considerable rise in lay Catholic activity seeking to reinforce 'family values', the sanctity of marriage, and views on contraception, divorce and sexual morality. Although formally part of the United Kingdom, Northern Ireland in many ways mirrored the Republic. Despite abortion and divorce being legal because of its link with the UK, such was the level of Catholic and Protestant observance that Northern Ireland retained a strong theocratic culture, as against the more profane and multicultural society of neighbouring Britain. Yet, despite this, considerable social change and politically articulated opposition to these kinds of tradition were expressed in the 1980s. Marital breakdown increased during the 1980s; increasingly people *did* exercise their individual consciences over the use of contraception, pre-marital and adolescent sex; and the decade also witnessed the emergence of lesbian and gay groups that challenged the heterosexual norms of society, north and south.

Economically, the 1980s saw both Irish states suffering severe recession and decline, and, with record levels of debilitating emigration – particularly of younger people – the lifeblood of change left the island. The economy in Northern Ireland was massively dependent on subventions from the Exchequer, and the Republic's economy was reeling from the withdrawal of multinational investments made in the previous decade. The Republic was becoming more integrated with the EU, finding new markets, attracting inward investment and becoming more engaged with European legislation (e.g. ratifying the Single European Act in 1987) in ways that sometimes challenged traditional views. Politically, the 1980s was a turbulent decade of political violence and many shifts of formal power. In the Republic, governments changed five times in ten years, providing little continuity of policy. Despite its emotional engagement with the political protest of the republican hunger strikers in Northern Irish prisons in 1980–81, the Republic tried to insulate itself from the Troubles, politically and mentally containing the problem. The political aftermath of the prison protests that ended with ten men starving themselves to death saw the rise and consolidation of Sinn Féin in Northern Ireland, but not in the Republic. The terms agreed in the Anglo-Irish agreement, signed between Irish and British premieres in 1985, angered unionists of all hues in Northern Ireland, who felt themselves bypassed by London.

The IRA had switched its attacks to targets in Britain and strategic British military targets in Europe, whilst Sinn Féin's Gerry Adams entered negotiations with the Social and Democratic and Labour Party (SDLP) through John Hume, the constitutional nationalist, in 1989. The late 1980s saw increasing divisions opening up between unionism and loyalism and a steady rise in loyalist paramilitary killings that outstripped the IRA. But if the beginning of the 1990s saw the end of Thatcherism in Britain and the election of Mary Robinson as a social democrat President in the Republic of Ireland, the heart of the political and cultural majority of Ulster Protestantism remained unexamined.

This is why, although it was a period film set ninety years earlier, *December Bride* had great social resonance and crucial political significance on its release in 1990. But the changes sketched out in the previous paragraph provide only one kind of socio-historical context through which to understand the film. It is equally important to understand the key features of the cinematic contexts that inflected themselves on the production of the film at this time. The idea for making a film of this novel came at a time of great uncertainty and instability in Irish film-making. Indeed, Britain and other European countries at this time were struggling to cope with Hollywood domination of the domestic box-office and to come up with strategies to revive national production and rescue ailing industries. With a long history of being represented in Anglo-American cinema, Ireland's indigenous film-making survived as a marginal and gapped tradition until the 1970s, when something resembling a critical film culture emerged. Meagrely funded, sporadically distributed, but fiercely championed, film-makers and their supporters successfully lobbied for state support for film, resulting in the establishment of Bord Scannan na Éireann/The Irish Film Board (IFB) in 1980, which existed practically between 1982 and 1987. During the 1970s and this period of the IFB, Bob Quinn, Joe Comerford, Cathal Black, Pat

5

Murphy and Neil Jordan established their reputations as film-makers of note and notoriety. Often innovative and experimental, their films carried a critical–aesthetic charge that explored topics and taboos in a rapidly modernizing and changing Ireland, a country in which social division and conflict were pervasive.

Their films not only worked to critique the traditions of nationalism, state and society in Ireland, but were also aimed at the largely foreign cinematic representations of Ireland that had dominated film screens. The recurrent and mutually dependent tropes of Ireland as a rural idyll, a past-centred place of escape from modernity and 'originary return' or as a dark zone of historic tragedy and ancient enmities were subjected to varying degrees of scrutiny. If this characterized an Irish 'Third Cinema',[7] it was not the purpose for which the state had envisaged providing public monies. It tended to favour a more commercially orientated cinema, made to larger budgets for audiences as much outside Ireland as within it. Given that the Republic was undergoing a severe financial crisis and that many film-makers were critical of state social and political policies, it is perhaps not surprising that funding for the IFB ceased in 1987. New tax legislation the same year provided incentives for foreign investment and many indigenous film-makers were left in a financial vacuum.

An unusual series of pressures then began to exert themselves on film-making in Ireland. Firstly, the new tax laws created a climate in which entrepreneurial Irish producers were encouraged to seek finance from outside of Ireland, looking in particular to the US and to British television companies with a track record of investing in film production. The kinds of film that emerged out of this period have been dubbed 'heritage cinema'.[8] They became synonymous with an international distribution of large-budget box-office and critical successe such as *My Left Foot* (1989) and *The Field* (1990). In Northern Ireland, in the virtual absence of any state funding for film-making during the 1980s (anomalously, not financed by the British Film Institute), the BBC and UTV had begun to dip their toes into film and co-production. This was a result of pressures within the UK industry to generate further income and to respond to the model for television/film symbiosis provided by Channel Four (established in 1982) as a commissioner of programmes and, more pertinently, a film production financier. The final component in a complex state of flux in Irish film was Europe. In what became a series of confrontations between the dominance of Hollywood in European cinemas and television schedules, a pilot programme of investment, support and collaboration between Member States of the EU was launched in 1987 under the banner of MEDIA92.

It is in this context that the Little Bird production company, with offices in London and Dublin, approached Thaddeus O'Sullivan in 1988 to direct a screenplay based on *December Bride*. Leaving Ireland in 1966, with great antipathy, and remaining at a remove from his home country, O'Sullivan was nevertheless crucially involved in the development of the critical film culture of the 1970s and early 1980s, although he has never seen himself as specifically part of this 'new-wave Irish cinema'. He learnt about film at London's Royal College of Art and produced experimental films like *A Pint of Plain* (1972) and *On a Paving Stone Mounted* (1978), which tried to express something of the Irish emigrant experience. He was lighting-cameraman on *Traveller* (Jordan/Comerford, 1982), *Anne Devlin* (Murphy, 1984) and *Pigs* (Black, 1984), and he also directed the acclaimed short *The Woman Who Married Clark Gable* (1985), itself an adaptation of a short story by Seán O'Faolain. With this kind of theoretical understanding and practical experience, O'Sullivan was critically aware of the dominant cinematic traditions of representing Ireland on screen (mentioned above), had seen a lot of European film in London – especially the films discussed in Chapter 3 – and was attracted to the *December Bride* project. It would be his first time directing a full-length feature, shot on location in a part of Ireland not normally visualized and based in the heartlands of Ulster Protestantism in County Down, a community that was under-represented in film.[9] From pre-release interviews, O'Sullivan clearly indicated an interest in critiquing the cinematic tradition of filming Irish landscape and questioning how Ulster Protestants had been portrayed in Irish cinema. In approaching David Rudkin to adapt the novel for screen, he was attempting to establish a break with trends in contemporary Irish film-making by adopting a northern European 'art film' aesthetic. In terms of finance and production, the project was just a little too early for MEDIA funding, and *December Bride* had to draw variously on television money from Channel Four International, UTV, Central TV and film money from British Screen. Thematically, the film suggested a timely reinvestigation of Ulster Protestant history and culture, and in particular the important claims of a tradition of radical independent thought and the socialism represented in the work of Sam Hanna Bell (discussed in Chapter 1).

Although there is evidence that Rudkin and O'Sullivan did not agree completely about all aspects of Bell's novel (see Chapter 3), it is clear that their combined creative talent in adapting *December Bride* produced nothing less than a critical reassessment of Sam Hanna Bell's significance to the culture and politics of Northern Ireland generally, and of Ulster Protestantism in particular. Along with films like *Hush-a-Bye-Baby* (Harkin, 1989), the film stands as a critical commentary on Irish society and politics in the 1980s, finding in the period setting a striking correlative for contemporary Ireland. In closing this introduction, it is worth reminding ourselves of the aims of the 'Ireland into Film' series. The treatment and creative motivations behind *December Bride* provide a suggestive case study and critique of much film-of-the book production and presents a richly consummate example of the process of novel adaptation itself.

1

THE NOVEL AND ITS CONTEXTS[10]

It is not just that Protestantism in Ulster is bound up with politics and culture, but that a religious upbringing establishes habits of mind which clothe the secular and, openly or secretively, the creative life.[11]

Heterodox Histories

In this chapter, Sam Hanna Bell's significance as a literary and cultural figure is assessed in the context of Ulster's history and the more recent writing traditions associated with Northern Ireland. Bell remains a key figure in a small group of 'progressive book men';[12] writers and cultural activists with non-conformist ideas whose work, taken collectively, represents an intellectual alternative to the kinds of unionism that dominated the political map of Northern Ireland in the twentieth century. Bell's activity and energy were prodigious. In the course of a long working life he was, amongst other things, a writer of fiction, a literary editor and a radio arts features producer (becoming the BBC's 'microphone in the countryside'). This chapter considers his début novel, *December Bride*, amongst his other work as the creative expression of a collective cultural politics which dissented from the formal politics of unionism that held sway during Bell's adult life. Bell's heterodoxy offered modes of identity that were at once popular and local, but which drew on international ideas such as socialism. His main purpose was to find a way to redefine the competing ideologies of Irish nationalism and the Britishness of Ulster Unionist politics that characterized his upbringing in Northern Ireland. In political terms, Bell's work may be seen to accommodate strains of a Scots-Irish dissenting tradition – with its non-sectarian expression in the 1798 uprising – and what became welfare socialism in the post-World War II period. The enduring significance of the novel is that it not only hit the mark in 1951, but that its publishing history delineates the changing contours of Ulster Protestant identity ever since. At key moments over the past fifty years, *December Bride* has found new generations of readers, has been reinvested with meanings and has provoked debate about the future of Ulster Protestantism. The filming of *December Bride*, I argue, is but another example of creatively 'remembering' the novel[13] in order to re-fashion politics and society.

Bell and Cultural Politics in Northern Ireland

It is ironic and significant that such an important figure in Northern Ireland's cultural history – especially its rural traditions – was actually born in industrialized Glasgow in 1909. The ties between Belfast and the Clydeside in the Edwardian period were based principally on shipbuilding and mill labour, with additional seasonal migrations of (mainly Catholic) workers to the agricultural hinterlands from Donegal via Derry. In fact, Bell's family life is emblematic of a well-established series of material, human and cultural connections between the eastern Ulster counties and the Scottish central lowlands that have shaped Ulster Protestant history from before the early seventeenth-century plantations.[14] Bell's father, James, had family roots in Scots-Antrim and Jane Bell (née McIlveen) was from Raffery, County Down, a village near Strangford Lough that provides the setting for the fictional Rathard in the novel and the shooting location of the film. Bell's early upbringing was subdued Presbyterian, middle-class and urban: his father moved up from being a merchant's clerk to becoming a journalist and newspaper editor. It is a feature of Sam's upbringing, as it is of many Irish in Great Britain, that summer holidays were spent with family relations in Ireland, and these early childhood visits made a deep impression: 'It was from that remote and idyllic past that I drew my novel *December Bride*.'[15] However, the

*Plate 1.   Sam Hanna Bell with actress Brenda Bruce on set in Strangford Lough
during the filming of* December Bride *in June 1989. Photo credit:
Dermott Dunbar. Courtesy of Blackstaff Press.*

untimely death of his father in 1918 meant that the Bells were subjected to an unseasonal, enforced return to the maternal homelands of Down. As Ruth Riddick pointed out when reviewing the première of the film, 'that early dislocation, a common element with many a writer, imprinted a townland, its life, customs and topography, like a photographic plate on his imagination'.[16] The Bells remained here for nearly three years until moving in with relations in Belfast, which reconnected Sam with an urban environment. But the impact of Down's strict Sabbatarian milieu, the heightened sensitivity to the rhythms of rural life and its folk culture, all fed into Bell's consciousness, resurfacing later in his early collection of short stories, *Summer Loanen* (1943), and the miscellany of recollections and lore titled *Erin's Orange Lily* (1956). These formative experiences, combined with his adult concerns as a writer and radio broadcaster, resurfaced during the writing of *December Bride* in 1940s wartime Belfast.

A lack of means probably denied Sam Hanna Bell the kind of secondary education that would have led him to university, but he was by all accounts an important figure in the constrained intellectual life of Northern Ireland in the late 1920s and 1930s.[17] He was an auto-didact among a small group of writers, teachers and political activists who explored the possibilities of socialism as an alternative to the established, opposing political ideologies of nationalism and unionism. Respectively, the first of these sought to assert Ireland's independence from the British Empire, whilst the other celebrated and valued the link. The temporary political solution imposed from London in 1920 involved the partition of Ireland, creating two parliaments: one in 1921 for 'Northern Ireland', eventually based at Stormont Castle near Belfast; one in Dublin for the 'Irish Free State' in 1922. These political institutions were the outcomes of the bitter ideological clash between 'Home Rule' nationalism (initiated formally by Isaac Butt in 1870) and Irish unionism (which had emerged in 1885–86 in reaction to Home Rule). The 'Ulster' character of unionism developed as a result of the mass organization of modern politics in the north, the infusion of evangelical zeal that swept through late-Victorian Ulster[18] and the commercialization of popular leisure activities.[19] Over a generation, key alliances were forged between unionism, industrial and British military interests and, crucially, the Orange Order, under the leadership of notable figures like barrister Edward Carson (a Dublin-born unionist). The popular commitment of unionists to Empire was indelibly reinforced with the sacrifice of the Ulster Divisions during World War I and its subsequent mythologization within Ulster Protestant culture.

Sam Hanna Bell shows in *December Bride* how popular manifestations of unionism and Orangeism were woven into the weft of urban and rural Ulster life at the turn of the last century. This can be seen not only in the scenes of 'The Field' (II. xvii) but also in the pub culture of Belfast (III. vii, in scenes cut out of the film). Although there were clear political and social affinities between the organization of unionism, Orangeism and Presbyterianism (the main Protestant Church),[20] it is important to signal that the elements of this 'bloc' were by no means homogeneous but contained class differences, urban and rural rifts, and theological conflicts. Nor was this bloc's hegemony unopposed ideologically. Firstly, writers and thinkers like Bell demonstrated that individuals and groups retained a strong sense of their autonomy and right to dissent from established authority. This deeply ingrained sense of libertarianism was a historical legacy dating back to religious and philosophical non-conformism in the seventeenth century.[21] Secondly, Bell seemed acutely alert to the fact that the rhythms and rituals of country life, attuned to the seasons and with its own pre-Christian folklore, offered an alternative set of traditions and ways of organizing people's lives that pre-dated the recent modernizing features of political and church organization. Thirdly, Bell championed an alternative history

Plate 2. Orange culture, rural landscape. 'The Field' sequence in December Bride *(1990). Photo credit: Simon Mein. Courtesy of Carlton Television.*

of Irish Protestantism which looked to the liberal, non-sectarian politics of the United Irishmen, a society founded in 1791 in Belfast and then Dublin. This middle-class grouping was largely Presbyterian and argued for religious toleration and independence from Britain. The United Irishmen stood for a radical republicanism, reflected in the popular (but failed) rebellion of 1798. They represented an alternative, pluralist republicanism, elements of which later generations of radicals could model themselves on. Bell and others tried to marry this historical 'legacy of difference and individuality'[22] with their contemporary circumstances in a partitioned Northern Ireland state where they experienced the domination of unionist politics and Orange culture as a stultifying reaction produced within a larger British imperial culture.

The Belfast that Bell moved to on the brink of his teenage years was a rapidly expanding provincial capital experiencing the growing pains of a new polity. Sectarian violence between Catholics and Protestants accompanied the partition of Ireland and the early years of government by the Unionist Party.[23] As a young man, he witnessed the growing singularity of the 'Protestant State for a Protestant People' in which Catholics became second-class citizens and Protestant nonconformists were politically invisible. The late 1920s saw the onset of a Depression that accentuated the thin 'privileges' of the Protestant working class, but it remained easy for unionists and Protestant church leaders to stir 'loyalty' by pointing south to the Catholicism of the 'Irish Free State'. Unemployment, poor social provision and political exclusion were the seed-bed for sectarian tensions that reached their peak in Belfast in the mid-1930s. However, the material and intellectual poverty of Northern Ireland caused people like Bell, John Hewitt and John Boyd to embrace socialism as a political ideal which was discussed vigorously in the Linen Hall Library, Davy McLean's socialist bookshop and Campbell's Café.[24] These and other writers, like Robert Greacen, Denis Ireland, Joseph Tomelty (a house-painter turned playwright) and the poet/broadcaster Louis MacNeice looked to the anti-authoritarian dissension of Ulster's past. In the immediate wake of World War II, some, like Hewitt – a lapsed Methodist with English planter origins from the 1600s – argued the case for Ulster's consideration as a distinct region, which complicated broad British/Irish identities. In an essay titled 'Regionalism: the Last Chance' published in 1947, Hewitt wrote of a regional identity forged 'out of that loyalty to our own place, rooted in honest history, in familiar folkways and knowledge, phrased in our own dialect'. From the region, he continued, 'there should emerge a culture and an attitude individual and distinctive, a fine contribution to the European inheritance and no mere echo of the thought and imagination of another people or another land'.[25] A self-styled dissident, Hewitt was expressing a complicated sense of disjointedness

15

that seemed all the more pertinent in the redrawn border areas of post-war Europe. The temporary status of the Irish border set up under the 1920 legislation was altered significantly at this time, with the unionist government under Basil Brooke negotiating Northern Ireland more permanently into the United Kingdom in the form of the Ireland Act (1949). This was possible because Éire's strategic neutrality in World War II and its secession from the British Commonwealth in the form of the External Relations Act (1948) were seen as strategically destabilizing. Making partition permanent helped to create a sense of stability and it was a political pay-off for Ulster's considerable part in the war effort. Yet, despite this move to unite the UK, the post-war period produced strong countervailing currents of regional expression and cultural work by working-class writers.[26]

Bell had spent the pre-war decade doing various menial jobs: in a potato merchant's, in the woollen trade, labouring in the Belfast docks, working as a night watchman, even working as a veterinary laboratory assistant. He wrote some children's fiction and occasional pieces on local folk traditions for the radio, and also edited *Labour Progress* in Belfast. During the war years, he was a reservist and an air-raid warden and contributed fiction to the Dublin-based periodical *The Bell* demonstrating his participation in the traffic of critical ecumenism in literature. His collection *Summer Loanen and Other Stories* was published by Mourne Press in 1943 and he co-founded a periodical called *Lagan*, a northern equivalent of *The Bell*, in the same year. He started working as a radio features writer in 1945 and then began a long career as a producer of programmes. According to Douglas Carson, 'Sam was a pioneer of the "outside" recording. At first on disc, and latterly on tape, he set out to democratize regional radio,'[27] by specializing in recording folk traditions, stories, recollections, and personal accounts of rural and urban trades and pastimes in people's own words, capturing their dialect and idiom.

Bell became a professional 'intellectual' via his position at the BBC, from which he articulated the history and ideas of a diffusely defined working class, although by and large he was not organic to the class with which he identified. His most significant contribution – outside of his own writing – was his work as a collector of material, an editor or commissioner of others' work and as a producer of radio and television features on Ulster life. Richard Mills' contention that his work should be 'read as an attempt to disinter a Protestant radical tradition and a rich, cultural, literary tradition – a tradition which is as native as any in Ireland' is a succinct summary of this view. He goes on to argue that 'in Bell's restorative project lay his radicalism; his regionalist examination was enough to query the accepted notions of Protestants as stolid and conservative, and to challenge the assumption that Ulster was culturally moribund'.[28]

Bell's Fiction: 'Between Love of Place and Experience of Change'

Bell's achievement as a novelist was shaped by the conditions under which he worked as a full-time broadcaster, resulting in what even one admirer termed 'the uneven quality of his inspiration'.[29] Yet Bell was a meticulous, painstaking and artisan author, crafting stories and novels over long periods, often interrupted by other editorial projects. If *Summer Loanen* was his apprenticeship work, then *December Bride* (1951) undoubtedly remains his masterpiece. He wrote three other novels over the next thirty years, each with a different historical setting. *The Hollow Ball* (1961) is set in the Depression years of Belfast and concerns the fortunes of David Minnis, a young man who is faced with the dilemma of choosing between a career playing football in England or remaining loyal to his roots and comrades in a woollen mill. The novel is the most obviously autobiographical of Bell's *oeuvre* and, according to one critic, 'reflects the tensions and divisions Bell was conscious of in his own life: between the active radical socialist of his youth and the bourgeois comfort of the BBC and marriage into the middle class'.[30] The other two novels are perhaps more pertinent to an appreciation of Bell's grander fictional project and the way that they link with *December Bride*. *A Man Flourishing* (1973) and *Across the Narrow Sea* (1987) form a kind of trilogy with *December Bride*, going back chronologically over the generations to the immediate post-United Irishmen period and the Scots plantation of Ulster of the early seventeenth century respectively. Both novels are historical romances, dealing with the notion of the lost opportunities of the past. *A Man Flourishing* follows the fortunes of young James Gault, his transformation from radicalism to respectability, a man caught up in the compromise and disillusionment which followed the 1798 rebellion and the formation of the Union. *Across the Narrow Sea* traces the travels of Neil Gilchrist from Scotland to Ulster in 1608. The rescue of a young heroine, Anne Echlin, at the end of the novel offers a line of family names that recapitulates Bell's earlier novel, *December Bride*. Although working retrospectively, Bell perceived these novels to constitute a trilogy, a fictional world based on historical facts, an actual geography of the past. They may also have acted as a creative examination of the tangled roots of his own family history. What comes across most clearly from Bell's fiction is an extension of his concerns as a broadcaster and editor. The wider cultural politics discussed above were developed in the inter-war period and in the immediate post-1945 years. His career can be read as a continuously elaborated creative response to shifting developments within Northern Ireland, and in particular to the inadequacies of the State, its iniquitous social structure and its moribund political culture.

Bell had lived the experience of two quite different eras and places, and the disjunctions produced by this 'return of the native' impelled him to construct a portrayal of the place and the people with which he was intimately yet problematically linked. Written during the 1940s

– a period of transition and terminus within Northern Ireland – Bell's retrospective purpose in *December Bride* was to express a sense of a distinct culture dying, of it passing away. It became, as he pointed out, 'a novel into which I poured all my nostalgic memories of a vanishing way of country life',[31] the more acutely felt because, although connected to it, he was not rooted in it. In its 'ability to build up a detailed, almost tangible evocation of place',[32] the novel is a fine example of what John Wilson Foster termed 'local naturalism' in Ulster fiction writing.[33] Bell takes great pains to ensure that the dialogue of his characters is authentically rendered in Ulster-Scots dialect, whilst the narrative prose has the cadences of his own expression. Yet, whilst the detail of rural life that Bell observed and treasured is wholly accurate, *December Bride* is far from being either 'museum-piece' fiction or a cosily-distanced view of country customs. It is a dynamic landscape marked by human intervention. Both contemporary and subsequent critics have likened Bell's work, and this novel in particular, to Thomas Hardy and his depiction of rural 'Wessex' in novels such as *Far from the Madding Crowd* (1874), *Return of the Native* (1878), *Tess of the D'Urbervilles* (1891) and *Jude the Obscure* (1896). There is an echo of *The Return of the Native* narrative in the fact that it features Damon Wildeve, an engineer-turned-publican who entertains a mistress (Eustacia Vye) while married to Thomasin Yeobright.[34] The *December Bride* scenario pushes this further, but Bell's preoccupation with love and mobility across class boundaries parallels that of Hardy's lifelong concern. There are also similar elemental and melodramatic strains to Bell's novels, including *December Bride*; and, as Raymond Williams has pointed out, Hardy, like Bell, occupied the uneasy border 'between custom and education, between work and ideas, between love of place and experience of change'.[35] My sense of the difference between the two writers is that Bell tries to give more agency to his main characters as they struggle for self-definition, whilst Hardy presents characters in a more passive, fatalistic way.

As co-editor of a miscellany called *The Arts in Ulster*, published in the same year as his first novel, Bell criticized the limitations of fiction writing in Ulster. He felt that as a body of work it had until then not fully expressed 'the deep tensions and collisions and arising syntheses underlying all vital communities'.[36] In *December Bride* Bell stressed the conflicts, tensions and change within a rural community by examining how it reacts to the actions of those who set up alternatives to accepted social customs and who defy religious conformity. It is Sarah Gomartin's defiant female sexuality and self-assertion, coupled with the principled independence of the Echlin brothers, Frank and Hamilton, that provides the most provocative topics of the novel (and the most attractive material for the film adaptation). The brothers are estranged from the community in the sense that they and their father exercise their freedom of conscience by believing in God but refuse to comply with the Reverend Sorleyson's strictures about *how* they observe that faith. They have also declined to join the Orange Order and for the most part have tolerable working relations with Catholics in the surrounding farmlands (II. iv.128–129).

In the novel, Sarah responds differently than her mother, Martha, to the situation in which they find themselves. On the Echlin farm Sarah transforms her servitude into security (pp. 63–64). The catalyst for her rebellion against her position in the social order is her assertion that Andrew Echlin's drowning accident was a self-willed sacrifice. Defying Sorleyson's religious interpretation of events, she then refuses to observe the Sabbath (pp. 41–44, 61–62), thus causing a rift between herself and Martha. After her mother's departure, Sarah embarks on a relationship with both brothers, spurred on 'by all the humiliating years when she was a girl' (p. 111). At its best, this 'unnatural arrangement' (p. 137) is as sexually and emotionally satisfying for the three involved as it is efficient and domestically practical for the farm (II. v). Its capacity to be personally disturbing – especially to Frank – is mainly due to the way that the *ménage à trois* is increasingly isolated by the community. The minister asserts that their set-up is an affront to the order of the 'countryside' (p. 137), by which he means against 'nature' itself and the human society of Ards, while it is also challenging in terms of theology, class and gender. Firstly, Sarah refuses to name the father of her children, to get married or partake in social rituals such as baptism, choosing instead to get him legally named a Gomartin (II. viii). Secondly, she works her way up from servant to equal partner in the economy of Rathard (p. 165), surpassing her female neighbours. Her feminine assertiveness gets her condemned by the locals as a 'shameless bisom' (p. 165) – meaning both a broom and an immoral woman – while at the same time she is an object of sexual fascination for men, including the frustrated Sorleyson. His mannered paternalism as a minister of religion masks an inner weakness and pathetic masculinity. When he makes a sexual advance she is more than a match for him and inverts his moral superiority to devastating effect (pp. 148–149). Sarah has intimations ('superstitions') that she might be called to account for her actions, but Bell makes it quite clear that she is driven to protect her life at Rathard 'for fear of returning to a life of drudgery' (p. 64), that she 'was fortified only by a secret stubborn shame and a hatred of subordination' (pp. 65–66), and that 'she had not done it designedly' (p. 165).

Over the years, however, the presence of the isolated alternative family *is* tolerated at a distance by the community and, treated as Hamilton's wife, 'Sarah was known as Mrs Echlin' (p. 240). Sarah is shown to take pride in the expansion of Rathard: 'By judicious purchases, several small neighbouring farms had been absorbed, and the Echlin property had moved forward and spread out like a pool that overflows' (p. 238). Contrary to Sorleyson's assertion of the 'unnaturalness' of the Echlin household, Bell's simile suggests that the relationship had in fact become 'naturalized'. Furthermore, while Bell's way of describing the changing ownership of the townland over

21

time invokes a naturally spreading image, he does not lose sight of human intervention as part of the natural cycle: 'harvest, and birth, marriage and *litigation* had changed the families in the farms' (p. 240, my emphasis). So Bell insists that humanity is a controlling force in a natural cycle, but that there is no guarantee that it will be exercised to progressive, re-distributive ends. Indeed, the potentially radical nature of Bell's female protagonist becomes incorporated into the larger economic forces of Ulster's 'rural capitalism'. Sarah's decision to marry Hamilton signals the taming of her gendered disruptions, albeit for the greater good of allowing her daughter to marry. In retrospect, Sarah's social mobility disguised less radical aspirations: 'Her desires were budding to fulfilment. A hearth, a home to preside over, the daily life of cattle and fowl in her hands, the desires of her own body' (p. 86). While it was against the social mores of the time to give her own name to her first-born son, it is significant that outside the solicitor's office she registers her own class aspirations by affecting a 'respectable' voice and manners (p. 155). While it is possible to offer a humanist interpretation of Sarah's acquiescence, the offer to finance her son-in-law's shop remains a thumping reminder of the bourgeois business values that she acquires and in which she revels (p. 284).

The structure of the novel – with its opening marriage of the elderly Hamilton and Sarah – is effectively that of an extended flashback, so we know from the beginning how the narrative will provide its own closure. The narrator suggests that Sarah does not absent herself from church out of principle, but rather out of the 'shame and remorse when she thought of the life that she was unrolling before the sight of God and her mother in Heaven' (p. 219). Bell has Frank killed in a building accident to 'punish' him for his part in the transgressive relationship (III. x), and as the novel proceeds Bell comments on his characters' behaviour: 'There was something drastically wrong with lives in which ambitions and passions were never disciplined nor checked except by external things' (p. 290). We can detect that 'stabilizing tendencies are already at work'[37] as the 'ancient shadows' emerge to haunt the farmhouse kitchen where Hamilton has agreed to marry Sarah. 'The faintest flounce to her step' (p. 299) suggests her youthful rebelliousness, but in Sarah we can see how the potential for a feminist challenge is recuperated by the forces of rural capitalism and social pressure. We should also note that Sarah's consciousness of class subordination does not preclude her from harbouring a deep-rooted sectarianism towards Catholics.

It is in presenting these contradictory features of individuals and in showing the dynamic interaction of people and place that Bell's strengths as a novelist lie. His novelistic preoccupation with the past, the rural landscape and its customs is derived paradoxically from his uncertain relationships with these things.[38] Bell sensed that the countryside he had visited as a youth had undergone profound modernization and cultural transformation by the time that he came to record his radio programmes and write *December Bride*. Not from Ulster but of it, a dis-placed Bell intensified 'place' in the novel in a way that struck a chord, from its first appearance and for subsequent generations, with 'native' readers, returned or otherwise, and particularly for Ulster Protestants who laboured to reach the point from which they could confidently write in the past tense of being 'once alien here'.[39]

The critical reception to the novel is neatly summarized in McMahon's biography of Bell.[40] Contemporary reviewers approvingly noted the literary comparisons with Thomas Hardy, but, as Welsh critic Raymond Williams acerbically noted, 'some metropolitan idiots still think of Hardy as a regional novelist because he wrote about "Wessex"',[41] overlooking the processes of change that both novelists encountered in their work (and which in Hardy's case led him to imagine a 'provincial future' that anticipated the cultural 'regionalism' of Hewitt, Bell and others).[42] Arguing a different line in a more recent essay, Anthony Bradley builds on the insight that, in Ulster Protestant writers like Bell, 'The imagination and art . . . are also shaped in positive ways by the spirit of Calvinism.' Coining the term 'Ulster Gothic', and specifically mentioning *December Bride*, Bradley goes on to open up a valuable line of argument, cross-referencing Ulster Protestant fiction with that of Hawthorne, Poe and Dickinson, 'constituting a sort of Northern Gothic, occupying an imaginative territory somewhere between Puritan New England and the Calvinist South'.[43] It seems to be the most critically fruitful approach to Bell's work to see his Ulster fiction in this interstitial mode, at the confluence of English and American literary traditions that were themselves markedly 'regional' in character, infused with a particular sensibility and, in Bell's case, rendered in a distinct Ulster-Scots dialect which formed the basis of a particular, emergent writing tradition. In an essay, tellingly titled 'A Necessary Provincialism' (alluding to a phrase from Hardy), Tom Paulin set Bell's work alongside three other writers from the North of Ireland. Paulin stresses the importance of writing that expressed the personality of rural place: 'In the cadences of their prose, they capture another of the accents of the country, a wry, soft, warm wisdom, a gentle humourousness'.[44] This for me epitomizes the characterization of Hamilton, especially as written for and realized by Donal McCann in the film version (discussed in Chapter 3). Moreover, the novel and the subsequent film's representation of a calmer, more moderate Ulster diction constitutes an important antidote to the hectoring bellicosity associated with popular media Free Presbyterians, most notably the Armagh-born Reverend Paisley.

A Novel After-Life

The book sustained a worthy after-life, having been championed since 1974 by Anne Tannahill, owner of the Belfast-based Blackstaff Press.[45] It is instructive to note that the front cover illustration for this new paperback edition featured a detail from a monochrome

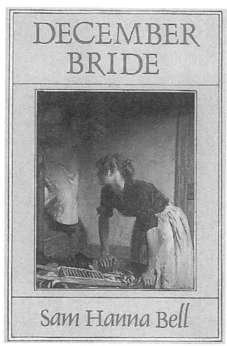

*Plate 3.   Front cover of December Bride
(1982): The first paperback edition.
Courtesy of Blackstaff Press.*

photograph of women working on a potato ridge in County Antrim
at the turn of the last century, thereby underpinning the 'authentic
naturalism' of the novel's depiction of life. The 1982 edition
continues the thematic focus on female labour by featuring a detail
from William Orpen's oil painting 'The Wash House' (1905),
depicting a woman bent over a washboard (see Plate 3). The 1989
edition (designed to coincide with the release of the film) comprises
a montage of Simon Mein's location photographs. Capturing the
essence of the film's narrative, Saskia Reeves as Sarah (in colour)
appears in period costume between the two brothers (Ciaran Hinds

Plate 4. Front cover of December Bride
(1989). Courtesy of Blackstaff Press.

and Donal McCann in monochrome, staring out of the picture). The three 'float' over a silhouette image of a horse ploughing against a skyline. Whilst the reference to rural labour is retained, the dominant image is of an assured young woman positioned between two older men. Their eyes share the same plane, but while the men stare out at us her gaze is haughtily off-glance (see Plate 4).

The novel's publishing history shows more than a passing correlation with moments of crisis and strategic rallying points within the politics of contemporary unionism and loyalism. The Ulster

Workers' Council strike that undermined the Sunningdale Agreement in 1974 followed the disestablishment of the Stormont parliament two years earlier. There were four reprints of the novel during the 1980s: 1982, 1983, 1985, 1989. The hunger strikes of 1980–81 grimly asserted republicanism as a political force in Northern Ireland for the 1980s, throwing down a challenge to the main constitutional parties: the nationalist SDLP, the unionist OUP and DUP, the liberal Alliance Party and also to the UDA (a politically organized loyalist group originating from Protestant paramilitary activists who by the early 1980s were espousing an 'independent Ulster'). The Hillsborough Agreement signed in 1985, by the Irish and British premiers in the absence of meaningful consultation with unionist MPs, provoked extreme anger amongst unionists, signalling in their eyes a 'sell-out' to Dublin by Westminster. Starting with no less than three reprints in 1990 alone, *December Bride* has been reprinted in 1991, 1992, 1994, 1998, 1999 and 2000. Buoyant sales may be attributed largely to the marketing power of the film, but the 1990s witnessed a decade of revived soul-searching, analysis and assertion of Ulster Protestant history and culture in the context of the Peace Process, which began in earnest in 1993. One liberal unionist commentator was moved to say at the time that he felt that, 'Unionism in Ulster today [1993] is like a body without a head, full of uncontrolled nervous functioning and lethal twitches.'[46] In such circumstances, interest in the novel and other Ulster Protestant cultural narratives reflect a popular and academic interest in re-membering, of putting the body of Ulster Protestant identity back together in a different form. *December Bride* is emblematic of this wider reconfiguration process, which includes Bell's work being taken up in part to generate a better understanding of Ulster Protestant culture in the Republic. By the end of the 1990s, *December Bride* had been anthologized and canonized as Literature.[47] The novel is now a prescribed text on the Republic's 'Leaving Certificate' syllabus in

English Literature. Here *December Bride* – the novel supplemented with the film version – addresses the burgeoning interest in media and cultural studies within Ireland and more general changes in the teaching of literature. It also potentially acts as a vehicle for Bell's tolerant and inclusive cultural politics to be encountered by younger students, though it is equally possible that positioning the novel as a 'set text' in a formalized syllabus may contribute to its radical energies being neutralized. Nevertheless, it is true to say that it was partly the emergence of this cultural politics which led Thaddeus O'Sullivan to take up the offer to adapt the novel when approached by the film production company Little Bird a decade earlier. And it is the cinematic contexts for the adaptation and production of the film that we turn to in the next chapter.

2

FILM PRODUCTION CONTEXTS

You select what you think is the essence of the book. But the process of adapting can be so reductive you have to be sure your choices establish an echo, in some way, with the complexity of the story. Choosing each location, for instance, was like adding back another echo of the book and the place it represents.[48]

Establishing an Echo

In this chapter we explore how *December Bride* came to be adapted into a screenplay and how this was produced as a film. Who was influential in making it come about and what were the kind of production decisions underpinning the finished film? O'Sullivan sees the adaptation task as one of selection, recombination and a necessary reduction in order to express the 'essence' of the novel and his memory of it, but also to recreate the ambience of the geographical locale represented in novel and film. When considering the intersections between art and commerce, between personal vision and collaborative effort, it is important to understand that *all* creativity is bounded and shaped by material conditions, whether it be writing a novel, making a film, or indeed in this case making a film based on a novel.

Accordingly, we examine the film's production in terms of individual creative processes and also broader institutional, economic and cinematic trends in the decade leading up to the film's production and release in 1990, and to the circulation period beyond. We begin with short profiles of the director Thaddeus O'Sullivan and the screenwriter David Rudkin, including their working relationship. What they produced constituted a radical reinterpretation of the novel, one that attempted to reconfigure Ulster Protestantism within Irish history. Rudkin insisted that in *December Bride* he wanted 'to help create a film that was authentically Irish, of an Irishness that simplistic nationalism or English liberalism can't quite accept'.[49] Key to this was their attitude towards the depiction of the countryside of County Down and how they interpreted Bell's fictional portrayal of rural Presbyterians, particularly in so far as, as film-makers, they 'seem to have absorbed some of the more attractive qualities that suffuse the way of life of their characters – a sober and chastened use of language whether in narration or dialogue'.[50] The practical issue for Rudkin and O'Sullivan was precisely this: to find an audiovisual language that was appropriate to the period material and to avoid certain cultural and cinematic clichés that were current in representations of Ireland up to that point. In this regard, O'Sullivan commented:

> I didn't want the look or feel of the film to be too familiar. That's always a danger with period stories. I wanted the Presbyterian life to feel different, not Irish, not particularly British either. I kept thinking of northern European film-makers like Carl Dreyer. David [Rudkin] and I talked about

the look and feel of his films, especially *Ordet* and *Day of Wrath*.

Their film sailed close to the wind but remained at the critical edge of an emerging trend that Ruth Barton has identified as 'Irish Heritage Cinema'.[51] Within the adaptation and production processes we can see that writer and director discovered similar issues to Bell working with fiction: the question of how to represent locale and tradition, how to tell a story in a dramatic, engaging way that does not trivialize or 'fix' the culture of its subject in a static way. There are parallels here with the discussion of 'regional' fiction in the last chapter, and the film shows a tension between a tendency towards a surface 'naturalism' and an attempt to find a deeper register that expresses the emotional and mental landscape of fictional characters in a real place. It helped that the writer, the director and the film's creative technicians (design and cinematography) were sympathetic to an aesthetic that was deliberate, spare and understated, a look and attitude that sought resonance with northern European art cinema rather than Anglo-American models. This general thrust can be found by considering the production process from pre-production location and casting to the activities of designing, shooting and editing the film. This chapter will identify a number of tensions within this process that will be teased out in greater detail for selected scene analysis in Chapter 3, particularly as they relate back to the novel. Through existing and new interview material, it is possible to outline how Rudkin and O'Sullivan found ways of expressing the relationship between their lived experience as long-term Irish migrants and their engagement with the matter of *December Bride*.

Visualizing the Inner Memory of Place

Originally from Dublin, Thaddeus O'Sullivan left Ireland in the mid-1960s with a secondary education, 'the last of the old-fashioned economic emigrants who left for good'.[52] He was a young man disaffected with what Ireland had to offer and, in London, after a period of manual labouring and office work, he successfully applied to Ealing School of Art to study graphics and design. However, he became interested in film instead and made an Irish ghost story in Celbridge, County Kildare, called *The Picnic* (1969). On the back of this, he applied successfully to the Royal College of Art in 1972, where he studied the theory and practice of film. *A Pint of Plain* (1975), his 'graduation piece', and *On a Paving Stone Mounted* (1978) were formally experimental and improvizational and were concerned with the fragmentary experience of emigration. He spent the late 1970s in the USA, working on script editing, short films and commercials. He directed a documentary called *Jack B. Yeats: Assembled Memories* (for RTÉ and the Arts Council in Ireland, 1981) and was director of photography for Jordan/Comerford's *Traveller* (1981), Pat Murphy's *Anne Devlin* and Cathal Black's *Pigs* (both 1984). A project to adapt John Banville's novel *Birchwood* did not materialize, but he was offered enough of a budget for a short film project. He hastily chose to adapt an O'Faolain short story, *The Woman Who Married Clark Gable* (with Brenda Fricker and Bob Hoskins), which was BAFTA nominated and, unusually for a short, was well-received on release in 1986 (with *Letter to Brezhnev*). He continued to do photography for television films like *On the Black Hill* and *Ladder of Swords* (both for Channel Four), and directed *Gold in the Streets* (RTÉ) and the adaptation *In the Border Country* (Channel Four, 1991). He was approached by Little Bird to direct an adaptation of *December Bride* in 1988. O'Sullivan has pointed out that he had been approached to do *December Bride* in 1983 by Strongbow, an Irish production company, but he did not like the script and turned it down.[53]

This second offer of a chance to film a novel that he 'loved' and was fascinated by could not be passed over. With offices in London and Dublin, Little Bird had a track record with Irish-related material, including *The Irish RM* (based on Somerville and Ross's popular fiction) and *Troubles* (a J. G. Farrell novel) for television, and *Joyriders* (1988) and *The Lilac Bus* (1990) for cinema. This list brings home the point made by O'Sullivan about how a director gets raw material for film. Aside from accepting scripts sent in 'on spec' or developing a story idea into a script with a known writer, the adaptation remains a staple source: 'It's the *main* option, it's what most producers do; books have ideas . . . as long as you can afford the rights'. On behalf of Little Bird's producers, Jonathan Cavendish and James Mitchell, O'Sullivan approached dramatist and screenwriter David Rudkin to see if he would be interested in taking on the rewriting of the screenplay owned by Little Bird (which they had originally commissioned from the Ulster novelist, Maurice Leitch). Rudkin felt the existing screenplay was both technically unredeemable and conveyed 'no emotional sense of the landscape either exterior or domestic, [the writer] had not tuned into the ethos, he couldn't "hear" the speech' (p. 1). This screenplay was a workmanlike job, but it was a literal, rather too 'faithful', transposition conceived for television rather than cinema exhibition. Little Bird were persuaded to commission Rudkin to write a new screenplay from scratch, which he did, writing longhand over a fortnight in June/July 1988 holed-up in a hotel in Wales.

O'Sullivan knew and admired Rudkin's 'pithy but poetic quality of writing' from having commissioned a screenplay, *Fool of the World*, based on Antonin Artaud's brief visit to Ireland, but this never found funding. Born in England in 1936, the son of a Protestant minister, Rudkin identifies himself as being of mixed '"Ulster stock": Irish on my mother's side, English on my father's', his father a minister of religion. Not unlike Bell's Ulster-Scots bifurcated belonging, Rudkin describes himself as being:

> brought up in an Orange family in the Birmingham Ulster diaspora; the farmlands and flax-fields and turf-scapes of

south Armagh and Tyrone were always the background 'home' in my mind . . . it was my grandfather's culture and from boyhood I knew it from within . . . [But] I was always problematized by my divisive heritage, whichever side of the water I was. (p. 2)

A dramatist for stage, radio and television since the early 1960s, Rudkin may be located at the critical fringe of a middle-class, establishment England. He had been classically educated, including Oxford, served his National Service in the Royal Signals and was a schoolmaster teaching music and classics in rural Worcestershire until 1964, since when he has lived in the Warwickshire countryside. Prior to the *December Bride* commission he had written several plays that featured Irish-related themes, notably *Cries from Casement as His Bones Are Brought to Dublin* (BBC Radio, 1973), *Ashes* (1974), *Across the Water* (BBC TV, 1983) and *The Saxon Shore* (Almeida Theatre, 1986). He was also an experienced screen and radio adapter and translator, having worked on several classical texts. O'Sullivan has commented that Rudkin's 'dialogue is spare, refined and the rhythm of his lines orchestrated with the most careful punctuation'. He also saw that Rudkin was instinctively in touch with rural life: 'He had a great sympathy for people who lived on the land and for the landscape too,' whether that be Warwickshire or the remembered landscape of his maternal grandfather.

Rudkin quickly demonstrated both his technical experience in screenwriting and a sensitivity to the cultural psyche of the world created by Bell in the novel. The major difference between Leitch and Rudkin's attitude towards the 'originary' material of the novel is signalled semantically on the title page of each script: Rudkin's is 'from the novel' rather than being 'based on' it and – as we shall see – both he and O'Sullivan collaboratively made a number of excisions, amendments and additions for their *December Bride*. The adaptation process is driven partly by trying to visualize the 'memory' of the

33

novel's impact on reading it. O'Sullivan has spoken of it as the book's 'echo', while Rudkin sees it as trying to capture 'what makes the *inner* meaning *visible*' (p. 2, his italics). It is instructive to quote further from Rudkin's own account of the adaptation process. His initial approach is:

a feminine way, by 'dreaming' the book in; then I take a masculine tack, analyzing and resolving the book itself, line by line, into all its elements, and ordering these into categories; then femininely again, I let all these components shift and transmute in my mind into things that I can 'see' on my inward 'screen'. (pp. 1–2)

For Rudkin, the adaptive process is dialectical and gendered. He has to imagine altered states of being, making himself experience the book in different ways in order to produce new combinations of visual images and make emotional connections with the material. Bell's subject matter provides us with a complex portrait of an Ulster Presbyterian woman at the turn of the last century and Rudkin's interpretation opens up the notion of a 'feminized' Presbyterian consciousness. We will see in Chapter 3 that – as a man – O'Sullivan was deeply engaged by, and wanted to explore imaginatively, the book's chief premise: the emotional possibility of a woman being able to love two men at the same time.

Rudkin's 'male' methodology involved using a set of coloured pens to indicate to himself the different elements, namely: visual details and moments (green), salient narrative details (blue), aspects of language and phraseology (black) and 'technical problems' (red). Working in this manner, he was then able to produce a 'continuity' first draft. Assuming the basic standard of one page of script equalling one minute of screen-time in the finished film, Rudkin's first draft was over-long at 124 pages. This draft was 'a fully developed document: technically you could budget it, cast it, film from it' (p. 2), but it is also (for Rudkin) an 'evolving' draft because it inevitably contains a number of 'wrong choices'. In consultation with the producers and O'Sullivan, Rudkin had managed by the fifth draft to get the script down to a more manageable 94 pages, or a feature film of just over an hour and a half. In between the first and fifth draft, the producers were going through the process of seeking financial investment to take the script beyond 'development' and onto the 'production' phase. The bulk of the film's finance came from Film Four International (the film investment wing of Channel Four Television) and Central Independent Television, but there was money also from British Screen,[54] support from RTÉ and a small amount from Ulster TV, attracted by the 'local interest' of the film. The script eventually went to eight drafts, but extra rewrites were also done via fax and telephone during filming the following summer.

With a workable script and most of the budget in place, Little Bird were able to go into pre-production mode, lining up essential technical and creative staff, getting O'Sullivan over to Northern Ireland to search out a series of locations, and starting the process of casting the main roles. *December Bride* had a relatively modest budget of £1.2 million (or $2.5 million)[55] and this set demanding limits to filming: 'We shot it very quickly over six weeks: four in the north and one in Dublin during the summer [of 1989] and then one week back up north in November to get the winter scenes.' O'Sullivan had explored the countryside around Strangford Lough using an Ordnance Survey map with the film's designer Adrian Smith, working out how best to use the surroundings to complement what Rudkin had suggested in his screenplay. Much of this reconnaissance was done from a motor boat on the tidal estuary. O'Sullivan took scores of photographs, researched historical sites and consulted the Ulster Museum. Half a dozen key locations were decided on to cover the rural scenes: the Echlin farmhouse on Island Taggart to the west of the lough; Granny Pentland's house on Mid-Island south of Grey Abbey; the tidal landbridge off Castle Island at the south-west of the estuary; Ravara chapel in a place called Garage; Agnes's cottage in Marlfield Bay, on the east of the estuary.

O'Sullivan's own heavily annotated map of the area still exists amongst the Little Bird production papers.[56] It shows that the locations chosen were devoid of obvious late-twentieth century landmarks ('no telegraph poles' is noted on the map) and the Echlin farmhouse was selected because the surrounding fields were still the 'old size (not opened up)'. But whilst the setting approximated to the period of the piece in this facile sense, historical accuracy was *not* the main impulse for the choice of location. Film-goers and critics may have been impressed by the apparent 'authenticity' of the scenery, but O'Sullivan himself 'didn't want to clutter the image with the unnecessary detail of naturalism'[57] and is actually resistant to that approach to filming landscape. It is important to understand that, rather than satisfying the needs of historical verisimilitude, the location setting serves an aesthetic agenda and performs a *cinematic* task. In the process of selecting, filming and editing the countryside, a number of cinematic deformations are made in this re-presented 'authentic' landscape, thereby changing actual distances, relations and the historic nature of sites. Thus, the film's Presbyterian church had been a Catholic church (but, because it remained consecrated, permission had to be sought for filming); in the scenes of the Twelfth of July, 'The Field' is actually the site of an historic hill-fort. For the purposes of this film, actual locations in the 'South' stand in for the 'North'. The short Belfast sequences were shot in the Stag's Head pub and Temple Bar in Dublin, and the boat accident sequence was shot in a tank at Ardmore Studios in Bray, County Wicklow.

These are not merely trivial details, but should alert us to the significance of production choices and the bearing that they have on our understanding of how, in a material sense, a film constructs its meanings for an audience. One final example will clarify this point further. The Echlin farmhouse was a careful reconstruction based on a run-down cottage on Island Taggart, chosen for its proximity and aspect in relation to the expanse of lough water. In the film, its isolation on a tidal headland effectively provides a strong visual metaphor of being cut off from the larger community of Ravara (see Plate 5). As already mentioned, the tidal causeway (an invention of the film; it is not featured in Bell's novel) is geographically further south, but the film 'sutures' the reality into a filmic representation of the separateness of the *ménage à trois*. Above all, in order 'to get a sense that the community lived on the fringe of their world', O'Sullivan 'chose locations where the landscape always met the sea [Plate 6]. The main characters lived on the edge of that community, so in almost every landscape shot you get a sense of their isolation.'

Thus it is possible to note the characteristic way in which the low hills surrounding the area are shot from the foreshore or vice versa, making each feature assume greater proportion and import to the

Plate 5.   Independence isolated. The memorable tidal causeway image. Photo credit: Simon Mein. Courtesy of Carlton Television.

Plate 6.   Thaddeus O'Sullivan on the foreshore of Strangford Lough. Photo credit: Simon Mein. Courtesy of Carlton Television.

narrative (see Plate 7). Clearly, this is a screen landscape that avoids just 'being a lyrical appendage' to the narrative.[58] As O'Sullivan commented: 'The lives of the three [main] characters are deeply affected by the landscape. It's not simply a backdrop. It has a lot to contribute and so locations were chosen with great care and photographed with that in mind.' This exemplifies how the director was 'on message' with his writer, since Rudkin has noted how landscape functions in his writing:

> [It] comes from what I have experienced landscape to be: the force that shapes the soul, and ordains the toil. The narrative landscape has always been one of the psychic sources of my work . . . I'm a countryman, in Ulster and in England, and I sense that to urban writers the landscape is a place *where*

Plate 7. Expressive framing and cinematography. Photo credit: Simon Mein. Courtesy of Carlton Television.

> things happen; whereas for me, landscape is a narratively
> determining presence . . . it *shapes* what happens. (p. 5)

Rudkin's writing and O'Sullivan's choice of how to film the land and
seascape seeks to represent visually their characters' marginal
existence. Landscape shapes their nonconformist, independent
mentality; it gives them a particular sense of being different. Whilst
the isolation of Sarah, Hamilton and Frank from the community is
clearly written into the novel and conveyed in the screenplay, the
visual metaphor of the 'causeway/island' was an inventive response on
the part of O'Sullivan and a significant addition to the script.

There are, however, dangers in emphasizing the 'organic'
relationship between landscape and character, one of which was that
the film might be misinterpreted as suggesting that characters were
wholly subject to their environment in a kind of ultra naturalistic
fashion. Martin McLoone has shown how the film clearly counters
such thinking by reminding us that the figures on the landscape work
it and conceive of it in economic not aesthetic terms.[59] O'Sullivan was
astute enough to realize that the photogenic (though largely
unfilmed) location, the use of local people for minor roles and as
'extras', the exacting period detail in the design and costume, and the
laconic Ulster-Scots dialogue, all conferred a quality of 'authenticity'
on the film:

> I was aware that it could look very naturalistic in its portrayal
> of farming life. Such beautiful landscape as you find around
> Strangford Lough could undermine what the film was
> saying. You had to be sure it was contributing to the story at
> some level.

Local press coverage of the filming noted that 'many of the film's
extras are locals, signed up to give the film an *authentic local
atmosphere*' (my emphasis).[60] Whilst the problem of 'authenticity' in

Irish culture[61] is encountered in Bell's novel (and his broader cultural project to collect folklore, document Ulster labour and pastimes, and help preserve a vanishing culture), O'Sullivan did not want his film to be seen as a celluloid 're-construction' of that life. The film does show rural life in great detail, but his aim in filming was:

> to manifest that on the screen in an un-fussy way . . . so that detail is in the scene, *but the scene is not about it*. The simplicity and the graphic thing is, it's important that you don't just let a designer overload the screen *with things that would have been there* and all of that. (his emphasis)

So whilst local historians and the Ulster Folk Museum were consulted regarding Adrian Smith's reconstruction of the cottage, the agricultural crafts and implements and Consolata Boyle's costumes, O'Sullivan was quite clear about his priorities:

> To show simply and not distract from the scene. I like getting the detail to work . . . how the house is painted or the way a piece of farm machinery sits in the haggard [yard], or the way a dry-stone wall has fallen. But you have to be careful not to overload the frame with stuff just because you think it would have been there in reality. I don't want the period thing to end up more important than what the story is about.

What is important to draw out of these two statements is that O'Sullivan is antipathetic to the kind of film or television realism associated with conventional literary adaptation. He is keen to emphasize that, as a director, in controlling the *mise en scène* of a shot or a sequence, his priorities are *dramatic* ('the scene is not about it') and *thematic* ('what the story is about'). He is concerned with the aesthetic question of how a film looks and what the audience experiences. For instance, conscious of the stereotype that Ulster

Protestants are uniformly 'dour' and that rural life was 'bleak', O'Sullivan explained that 'the costumes are as colourful as we could make them [. . .] to give a richness to their lives. Not just to make the film more watchable but to put a gladness into it.'[62] Similarly, O'Sullivan was aware that the local dialect would complicate the audience's preconceptions about what an 'Irish' screen accent sounds like. As one reviewer noted, 'The unique accent in the area [is] a long way from what is traditionally regarded as the Irish brogue.'[63] O'Sullivan argued that the variety of accents within Northern Ireland is not fully appreciated in Britain and that regional distinctiveness is often misconstrued: 'The British [sic] have a funny attitude to Northern Irish accents, they don't realize how beautiful they can be and how these people use it to express their real selves'. O'Sullivan's task – indeed any director's – is to resolve a complicated, collaborative problem. The choice and direction of the actors, the lighting and camera work, the pace of the editing and the mood of the incidental music are activities carried out within limits of space, time and budget. These 'limits' present difficulties but also provoke creative responses to how a film is realized. *December Bride* was a small-scale (£1.2 million) production shot with a tight-knit crew over two intense periods totalling six weeks in May/June and November 1989. In O'Sullivan's view this helped to create the sense of it being 'utterly organic, really rooted, and concentrated in terms of location in relation to camera'. The finished film conveys an understated, slow-burning, absorbing narrative, but the work to produce this did not take place in self-defining isolation, even though it may have felt like that during production on location (see Plate 8). O'Sullivan was clearly trying to articulate his ideas about the drama of the unconventional relationship that lies at the core of the film. On one level, this focus is explained by his personal motivation to explore the dynamics of the *ménage à trois* at the heart of Bell's story:

Plate 8. *Thaddeus O'Sullivan (left) directs Donal McCann and Saskia Reeves during an intense period of filming on location. Courtesy* The Down Recorder.

In the novel I liked the story of Sarah's love for the two men. I can't say it's ever happened to me but I like to believe that there are some people who have the capacity to be absolutely in love with two people at once.

In the film, much of the broader social sweep of Bell's novel, several sub-plots, excursions and elaboration of detail are reduced in favour of this concentration on the dynamics of the triangular relationship, and this is discussed more fully in Chapter 3. O'Sullivan developed this point about the nature of human love and explained that he wanted to explore this lesser-known landscape of the emotions:

When you fall in love, isn't it because that person echoes you in so many ways? Can you be rational about it and decide

> you love one person for certain reasons and another for
> different ones entirely?

It is perfectly valid to consider O'Sullivan's comments at this personal
level, but there is clearly a social and political context for his
exploration of the theme. Furthermore, it is also fruitful to historicize
this as part of a complex debate in Ireland during the 1980s focusing
on heterosexual monogamy ('marriage' and 'the family' often
standing in as *the* ideal models here) and cinematic representations
of Irishness. At the time of its release it is interesting therefore to
recall a comment by O'Sullivan:

> I didn't want the film to look in anyway Irish or British, in
> terms of casting, the way it was written, the look of it, the
> framing of it, the colour of it, anything . . . I also wanted to
> position the film in a northern European context, visually
> and culturally.[64]

That an Irish-born director living in London should desire to have
his film look neither 'Irish' nor 'British' but 'European' is explored
in the following section and in the next chapter.

Contemporary Irish Cinema: Anglo-, American, European?

Although he did not want it to 'look' it, the empirical evidence shows
that *December Bride* – from its writing and funding, to its production
and distribution (not to mention its casting) – was precisely Irish and
British. Perhaps because the positive aspiration to attain a 'European'
aesthetic is so strongly accented, the unspoken absence in his
formulation is 'American'. However, Martin McLoone's idea that
December Bride contains ironic allusions to John Ford's *The Quiet Man*
certainly has no basis in the director's conscious intentions (and only
passing textual evidence), but the broader argument that the film is
attempting to run against the prevailing Anglo-American cinema

images of Irishness has better foundation.[65] While O'Sullivan did subsequently engage with popular American genres (for example, the gangster pictures *Witness to the Mob* [1998] and *Ordinary Decent Criminal* [2000]), my argument here is that, in this case, rather than counter Irish-American stereotypes with ironic play, he was more concerned with positively adapting an Irish literary text to draw on traditions within European art cinema. This was not only because it seemed a more appropriate treatment of the material but because it allowed him to subvert the traditional representations of Ireland and the Irish in the process.

In seeking to make and market the film as art cinema within contemporary Europe (it was distributed by the British Film Institute, a state-funded national institution), O'Sullivan and the Little Bird producers were contributing to a wider trend during the 1980s which, according to one prominent critic, saw 'art cinema' (increasingly funded by television) become pre-eminent within British film-making.[66] Thus O'Sullivan's desire to work within a set of visual and narrative conventions which he considered alternative to those commonly associated with Irish or British cinema may be qualified but not entirely invalidated, and turns instead on his status as a creative migrant.[67] It is not an unknown feeling for someone in O'Sullivan's position to resist *both* the negative no man's land of being termed an 'Irish-director-in-exile' or being dubbed as one who has silently and unproblematically assimilated himself into the British 'industry' network of independent production. The creative response to embrace an 'imagined' European identity might, ironically, be a crucial index of a particular kind of postnationalist Irishness of a long-term emigrant.[68] Drawing on a variety of cinematic historical influences, from the *nouvelle vague* movements of French (Varda, Truffaut), Danish (Dreyer) and Swedish (Bergman) film in the 1960s to more contemporary Danish film-makers (Axel), O'Sullivan was conscious that 'it was almost like I kind of imagined European cinema' (see Plate 9). Indeed, the academic literature about the nature of European cinema shows little consensus and, as Chris Darke has noted, 'the specificity of European art cinema is increasingly unclear'.[69]

This qualification aside, there are a number of traits associated with the term 'European Cinema'. The films produced for this cinema are characteristically small to medium budget, often funded partly with state support, with a small production team that privilege the writer and/or director's control and self-expression. Art cinema invariably presents *auteur* films in which classical continuity editing takes a back seat to stylistic, expressive qualities in the *mise en scène*. Which tends to promote ambiguities and unresolved ideas rather than narrative closure. Unlike Hollywood narratives, the art film

Plate 9.   Cinema as art. Donal McCann and Saskia Reeves. Photo credit: Simon Mein. Courtesy of Carlton Television.

tends to be driven less by action and plot and more by character dilemma. Dramatic conflict in the art film is typically generated by internal, psychological angst or by the way in which society affects character, but art films tend not to offer political analysis. European art cinema is usually defined by its small-scale, local setting and its stress on vernacular language and cultural expression. It is typically associated with the 'new waves' of national cinemas in post-1945 European countries, although its historic roots go back to cultural movements and experimentation with film in the 1920s. Since the late 1980s, art cinema films have tended to be seen simplistically as national–cultural bulwarks against the popularity of Hollywood films in European cinemas. But, as we have indicated with *December Bride*, art cinema is quite capable of interrogating and complicating unitary notions of national identity.

This chapter has developed an argument that has led us from the individual and collaborative ideas of screenwriter and director, to understanding the production and economic contexts of *December Bride*. We have also discussed the broader cultural contexts of a European art cinema in which the film was realized at the end of the 1980s. In considering the different aspects of the film's production in this chapter, we referred to a number of film-makers from an *auteur* tradition who have been influential on O'Sullivan. At this point, recall that in Chapter 1 we situated Bell's novel intertextually within the regional literature of English and American traditions, from Hardy to Poe, as part of a discussion about the heterodoxy of Ulster Protestant history and culture. We start Chapter 3 with an examination of the cinematic intertextuality of O'Sullivan's *December Bride*, looking at the thematic and formal properties of selected films from historic and contemporary European cinema.

3

MOVIE MATTERS: INTER-TEXTS AND TEXT

A film I saw as a teenager fascinated me – Agnès Varda's Le Bonheur
*[1965]. For a good Irish Catholic, there were several exciting notions to
contemplate here . . . When I read Sam Hanna Bell's novel . . . I had not
expected to be reminded of that film.*[70]

Cinematic Intertextuality

The main thing about the novel that excited O'Sullivan's mind 'was
wondering what it was like for a woman to be in love with two men
at the same time'.[71] But in order to understand the intrigue we need
to consider the intertextual nature of *December Bride* in more detail,
examining how it manifests itself in the finished screen text. To do
this we need to consider some key films from European art cinema
on which O'Sullivan and Rudkin consciously drew to adapt the basic
narrative provided by the novel. Borrowing themes (such as the
ostracization of individuals – especially within religious
communities), adapting characterization and narrative conventions
(such as triangular emotional and sexual relations) and imitating a
stylized *mise en scène*, O'Sullivan, Rudkin and the creative group that
formed the production team were able to construct a matrix of
references in which to situate their interpretation of the novel.
Finding a visual register for the film and a set of thematic parallels
was an important cinematic complement to the material. It was also
integral to offering the alternative view of Ireland on screen – and of
Ulster Protestants in particular – discussed earlier in this book.[72]

Just as coming to the film of *December Bride* having read the novel
makes for a richer viewing experience, knowing the cinematic
traditions in which the film is steeped may also bring other valuable

contexts to our understanding of what it is we are watching. Extending the point about textual interdependency outlined in the Introduction, we can argue that *December Bride* exists in *inter*dependent relation to traditions of European art cinema, however problematically constructed that notion might be. At the end of Chapter 2 we briefly outlined some of the traits of art cinema and in this section these are exemplified, even though the range of film-makers alluded to stretches across several decades, from Carl Dreyer's *Day of Wrath* (Denmark, 1943) and Agnès Varda's *Le Bonheur* (France, 1965) to Gabriel Axel's *Babette's Feast* (Denmark, 1987). Although we have noted that there was no European finance in *December Bride*, there was considerable involvement of continental European talent in the film's production. Perhaps the most significant and memorable element in the film is the cinematography of Bruno de Keyzer, a Frenchman who had photographed *Babette's Feast* and whose work is closely associated with the films of Bertrand Tavernier. The film's music score was written by the German composer Jürgen Knieper, whose work O'Sullivan had overheard in an editing facility in London while working on another film. The film's 'European-ness' is not only signified in historical, aesthetic and production terms, but through a consideration of the strategic release, promotion and critical recognition within the circuit of festival and art-house screenings. Most notable was its selection for the Quinzaine des Réalisateurs (Directors' Fortnight) at Cannes in May 1990, but also a Special Jury prize at the European Film Awards that year in Glasgow at the suggestion of its Chair, Swedish director Ingmar Bergman.

The point here is to place such cross-referencing alongside a consideration of the film's release in Ireland and Britain in 1990–91, particularly its coincidental appearance with films like *Hush-a-Bye-Baby* (Margo Harkin, 1989). These lower-budget films shared a platform at the Dublin Film Festival in March 1990 and circulated as a 'counter-cinema' to that of Jim Sheridan and the Anglo-American presence of mainstream, star-vehicle films such as *The Dead* (1987), *High Spirits* (1988), *My Left Foot* (1989) and *The Field* (1990). A consideration of the film's theatrical circulation in Ireland, Britain and further afield confirms its art-house positioning. Whilst *The Field* played at the Savoy, O'Connell Street, and one of Dublin's first multiplex cinemas, *December Bride* was itself doing record-breaking business at the Light House in Middle Abbey Street, one of Dublin's few art-house cinemas (since closed) (see Plate 10). It is important here to signal that O'Sullivan, whilst he knew and admired Harkin's film, did not see his own film as forming a conscious critique of the conservative turn and the containment of dissident voices in Irish society during the 1980s.[73]

Finally, this chapter concludes with a series of analyses of selected scenes and sequences from the film, looking in detail at the transformations brought about in the adaptation process from novel to screenplay to the final screen version. As has already been indicated, there were differences and tensions in the collaboration between writer and director over certain sequences and scenes. These are discussed because they are crucial to the interpretation of the novel and because they allow us some insights into the adaptation process itself.

Love Triangles in European Film: 'Not a Rustic *Jules et Jim*'

One of the chief functions of narrative in the heyday of classical Hollywood cinema was to represent 'heterosexual romance' leading to marriage and family as natural and normative modes of human existence.[74] Variations to this could be acknowledged but were invariably figured as deviant and usually seen as characteristic of another kind of 'foreign' cinema, usually 'European'. Although this heterosexual patriarchy was subsequently challenged from within by feminist, independent US and so-called 'queer' cinema, western

"MARVELLOUS . . AUDIENCES ARE IN FOR A REAL TREAT."
Nicholas O'Neill — Sunday Press

"STUNNINGLY BEAUTIFUL. THROBS WITH FEELING AND PASSION."
Ciaran Carty — Sunday Tribune

"ONE OF THE
BEST IRISH FILMS
EVER MADE."
Anna Coogan
Evening Herald

"TRULY A
BRILLIANT
PIECE OF WORK."
Mary Moloney
Evening Press

"SASKIA REEVES
IS PERFECTLY
CAST. SPLENDIDLY
CONVINCING."
Paddy Woodworth
Irish Times

"POWERFUL
PERFORMANCES
BY DONAL McCANN
AND CIARAN HINDS."
Ronan Farren
Sunday Independent

DECEMBER
—BRIDE—

A LITTLE BIRD PRODUCTION   Directed by THADDEUS O'SULLIVAN

DONAL McCANN · SASKIA REEVES · CIARAN HINDS

FROM FRIDAY
NOVEMBER 23

 LIGHT HOUSE CINEMA MIDDLE ABBEY STREET ☎730438

2·15, 4·15, 6·15, 8·30
(Sun.: 3·30 & 8.15) 15s

Plate 10. Publicity for release of December Bride *at Light House Cinema, Dublin (1990). Courtesy* In Dublin *magazine.*

cinema remains dominated by a Hollywood that has shown itself well able to recuperate 'deviant' desires of different kinds and market them in the mainstream with remarkable facility. Contemporary, European-produced (often US-funded) films have also shown themselves capable of using narrative conventions such as the triangular love contests between two men for the attentions of a woman. Taking an Irish example, the testing of male friendships (and attendant suggestions of latent homo-eroticism)[75] is central in a film like *Michael Collins* (Jordan, Warner Brothers, 1996), in which the eponymous hero and Harry Boland compete for the affections of Kitty Kiernan in a romantic sub-plot to the main epic narrative of the nation. In *December Bride*, the conventional romantic interest is suggested between Sarah and Fergus. Following her visit to the Pentland farm with the Echlin men to fetch the ram, a possible romantic pairing is confounded by Sarah's growing relationship with both the Echlin brothers – much to the chagrin of Fergus.[76] Instead of the Hollywood competitive 'romantic' triad model, the nature of the 'triangular love' alluded to cinematically is of a different class altogether. It is sourced from notable films of the French *nouvelle vague* and other national cinemas of Europe in the post World War II period, in which romance, marriage and family provoked angst-ridden questioning rather than reinforcing social norms and stability.

However, apart from the central character's espousal of a sexual love for two women in *Le Bonheur*,[77] it is not immediately obvious why Thaddeus O'Sullivan would be reminded of his viewing of this film in the mid-1960s when he later read the novel of *December Bride*. He observes that Varda's narrative, with a central male character – François, the provincial carpenter, happily married to Thérèse, who falls in love with a post office clerk – is qualitatively different from Bell's Ulster scenario, which has a woman at the apex rather than the base of a love triangle. Indeed, whilst Varda is one of the few French female film-makers of note to emerge from the *nouvelle vague* and feminist politics of the late 1950s, her feminism is of an independent, nonconformist nature that has confounded some feminist film theorists.[78] But it is a simplistic reading of *Le Bonheur* that objects to the way in which Thérèse is killed off at the end of the narrative to make way for the lover, Emilie. Rather, the luminescent palette and brightness of the cinematography, the highly stylized use of colour and the Mozart music score 'mismatched' with contemporary French life are all devices that stress the heightened non-realism of the film (see Plate 11). Indeed, the apparent ease with which 'wife' is replaced by 'lover' to take over the 'mothering' of the children suggests a feminist analysis of underlying social structures. Varda's film shows

Plate 11. Le Bonheur *(1965). François tells Thérèse he also loves Émile. Courtesy of Cine-Tamaris.*

that marriage as an institution and 'family life' as an ideal serve a broader ideological purpose. Based on Christian heterosexual monogamy, these structures cement the existing social fabric and individuals enmeshed in it are effectively replaceable elements. 'Happiness' (*le bonheur* – literally, good time) in Varda's film is underscored by this critique which is built into the film's text and which produces the unnerving quality of a non-voyeuristic viewing experience.[79] Note also how, in the recurring scenes of 'bliss' in the forest, linking nature to what is a *social* process of human interaction and not an 'escape', it is similar to Bell's use of imagery in his novel (Chapter 1 above). Although François philosophizes about the capacity to love more than one person, his liberalism of the spirit does not extend beyond marriage/lover relations, and his wife is presented with a *fait accompli*. In this regard, *December Bride* offers a scenario of a working, mutual and public *ménage à trois* in which 'the three of them were happy and looked into each other's eyes when they spoke' (79). It further offers an alternative parenting and 'family' model that has more in common with another classic French new wave film which explored similar territory (though with less radical conclusions).

François Truffaut's *Jules et Jim* (1961), an adaptation of a novel, pre-dates Varda's film and is different in many respects. The film tells the story of two young intellectuals in Paris, Jules (an Austrian) and Jim (a Frenchman), from the turn of the century to the end of World War I and its aftermath. Shot in black and white, it features film techniques and an attitude to its period material that are emblematic of the freshness and daring of the *nouvelle vague*. Thematically, it features a *ménage* involving Jules, his wife Catherine, and Jim. This arises when, despite Jules and Catherine having a daughter, Sabine, they realize that their love is more of an intense friendship than a shared passion. Jim it turns out had always harboured a secret love for his best friend's wife and, rather than see Catherine disappear with another lover, Jules consents to his best friend 'moving in'. The *ménage* in the countryside is short-lived, however; Catherine remains unstable and, even though she becomes engaged to Jim while they try for a child, Jim is also still emotionally involved back in Paris. The film is centrally concerned with the different ways in which two men love a magnetic and powerful woman, although, in its milieu, technical experimentation and tragic resolution (Catherine deliberately kills herself and Jim by crashing her car), it contrasts markedly with *December Bride*.

The films of Bergman and Dreyer provided the northern European influences for Rudkin and O'Sullivan both in thematic and cinematic terms. Ingmar Bergman's *Through a Glass Darkly* (1960) explores a dysfunctional family (David, the father, and his two children, Karin and Minus) staying on an isolated island in the Baltic Sea, trying to recover from the death of the children's schizophrenic mother. The seventeen-year-old Minus is unable to connect emotionally with his father, a preoccupied writer and grieving husband. Ominously, Karin also suffers from a form of mental illness and hears the voice of God in her head. Left alone one day, Karin sexually seduces her brother – providing him with a warped form of the love and attention he seeks – before receding into insanity and being helicoptered away, leaving the son and father apparently but unconvincingly closer. Despite its shaky conclusion, the film's artful composition heightens its thematic concern with the nature of religious faith and intense (sometimes taboo) forms of love. As such it provided a cinematic alternative for framing an Ulster narrative such as Bell's with similar mental and geographical contours.

Carl Dreyer's *Day of Wrath* (1943) is set in seventeenth-century Denmark within a tightly-knit, isolated rural community closely supervized by its religious elders – a scenario that finds immediate resonance with Bell's townland of Ardpatrick. *Day of Wrath* maintains two parallel plotlines, one of which remains unresolved at the end of the film. The first involves the accusation, torture, trial and execution of Herlofts Marthe for being a witch. Early on, she tries to seek sanctuary with a pastor, Absalom, and his new and much younger wife Anne, who live with his mother, Old Merte, in a state of domestic tension. It seems that, in this clutch of films, mothers are highly significant figures in the narrative: whether alive or dead, their presence is felt. In this case, we learn that Absalom and his first deceased wife had had a son, Martin, who returns home from university only to fall in love with his new 'mother' Anne (see Plate 12). Several hints in the film suggest that Anne herself may be a witch – not least of which is the fact that she seems able to will her ageing husband to drop dead. The triangle between Absalom, Anne and

Plate 12. Taboo triangular desires. Day of Wrath/Vredens Dag *(1943). Courtesy of Paladium Films.*

Martin (see Plate 13) involves an 'incest' taboo, but this forbidden desire is ambiguous: it might be 'true love' or the result of Anne's witchcraft. The falling 'in love'/'under a spell' process is signified in a variety of ways, the most interesting of which are the sequences in the countryside (which recall our discussion of Varda's use of the forest, and indeed *Jules et Jim*).

A later Dreyer film, *Ordet* (1954), features an isolated, rural Protestant farming community, set by the sea. The cinematography of this windswept landscape provided a template for O'Sullivan in conceiving the look of *December Bride*. In terms of narrative, *Ordet* (meaning 'the word') features two families so divided by a religious schism that a son is barred from marrying into the other's family. The son's mother, Inger, is expecting another child but dies in labour (as does the child), despite the assistance of the complacently 'modern'

Plate 13. Son/lover, Mother/lover. Day of Wrath/Vredens Dag *(1943). Courtesy of Paladium Films.*

doctor and presence of the local pastor. Throughout this, the family's eldest son, Johannes, is mentally distracted and wanders about the household acting as if possessed by the Holy Spirit. He is only politely tolerated by his family during the crisis of his mother's ill-fated labour and the villagers think him an unfortunate crank. However, in a strangely emotional climax to the film, he performs a miracle at his mother's funeral and brings her back to life, and as a consequence the two families are reconciled and the next generation can marry.

Both of these Dreyer films are drenched in (and structured by) biblical language and screen imagery. Encompassing the social conflict produced by proscribed passions, differences and doubts within religious faith, the films suggest a broader tension between orthodox Christianity and professional medicine on the one hand, and folklore/witchcraft and unorthodox faith on the other. This theme has a minor correlative in Bell's novel in the form of Agnes Sampson, the local herbalist, midwife and wise old woman (pp. 52–57, 242), and at one point in the film Frank remarks (as he takes her herbal cure): 'Time was, Agnes, they'd ha' burned ye for a witch that you are.' To which she replies, matter of factly: 'There's them'd burn me yet.' *Day of Wrath* and *Ordet* may both finish decisively, with a death and a resurrection respectively, but both are open-ended, ruminative and metaphysically questioning films whose stark, spare settings are richly symbolic and ambiguous. The elliptical qualities of the dialogue and intensely allegorical narratives expressed perfectly Dreyer's radical self-doubting mindset. Rudkin's style of screenwriting found an effective cinematic correlative with which to render the fictional Ravara community of Bell's novel. Sarah's defiance of her minister's moralizing interpretation of Andrew Echlin's death is a catalytic moment in the film (and indeed the novel, I. v. 41–44). She sees it as an act of self-willed sacrifice rather than an exemplary divine intervention to test the fortitude of mortal faith. The resilience of independent thought, the defiance of convention and the refusal to accept authorized dictatorial religion are common themes explored in these films. They also have strong parallels with *December Bride*, as we shall see when we explore the film text in more detail.

Returning to Texts: Selected Scene Analyses

In this final section, we examine selected scenes from the film, comparing different draft versions of Rudkin's screenplay to Bell's novel. A number of scenes and details from the novel differ from the finished film but do not alter its essential shape. So, for instance, in Part I Hamilton and Sarah's visit to Belfast (xii) is much reduced in the film, focusing on a growing intimacy that culminates in sex in the cart. The film indicates this but cuts away (it was issued with a '15' BBFC certificate), whereas, for its time, Bell's descriptive prose is quite explicit (pp. 99–100). Other details, such as Frank and Purdie fixing a water-wheel (I, xiii), Frank's bee-keeping, the sugán (straw-rope) making (II. v) and in Part III the mechanized threshing, are all dropped, probably for reasons of space but also because the crafts and rural economy were already sufficiently conveyed. Sarah's trip to Ardpatrick (II. viii) to register Andrew with her surname is truncated, so that we do not hear her use the name 'Gomartin' until the confrontation with the brothers when they move Bridie Dineen into Martha Gomartin's old cottage. It is the second half of the book that receives the most severe editorial treatment in the adaptation process. Scenes of young Andrew's upbringing, the threat of whooping-cough, his deafness and the social stigma of being a 'by-blow' (illegitimate) are all excised (corresponding to II. xi–xiii, III. ii in the novel). In the novel, Hamilton reacts violently to Tammie Gilmore's (II. xviii) verbal abuse and gets shot in the shoulder for his trouble. Excising this incident furthers the film's portrayal of Hamilton as not only a tolerant but a non-violent individual.

All of the childhood of young Martha (III. I) – until she starts courting Joe Skillen – is cut, and even this is heavily truncated (III.

vi–ix). All of the sub-plot of Old Petie's cattle-drive to Belfast (III. vii) and the melodramatic conclusion of this chapter (p. 270) are excised from the film. This was chiefly to focus on and intensify the key narrative ramifications of the *ménage* and Sarah's impending decision to marry and allow Martha 'a name'. It also has to be admitted that the film's budget constraints had a bearing on these decisions. Much of this excised material constitutes the novel's rich documentation of social life but its inclusion would have obscured the sharp lines of the central dramatic dilemma, and would have cost a great deal more to put on screen.

There are a number of other scenes invented by Rudkin or O'Sullivan that take a hint from the novel (a line or an image) but go on to become notable screen moments. For example, Sorleyson's attempt to enforce his stock Presbyterian view of the irregular, immoral nature of the Echlin *ménage* and the child's unresolved paternity is one of the central conflicts of the narrative of *December Bride*. In the novel (II. v) Sorleyson confronts Sarah, then the brothers, but the chapter concludes with the minister in disarray: 'He could not capture his mood of righteous disapproval . . . He envied them. These people had grasped what he had always secretly longed for' (p. 138). While Sarah tends the baby in the kitchen, Sorleyson upbraids her for not knowing who the father is, and for refusing to marry either brother for the sake of her 'good name'. Sarah asks, 'What ails my name?' and, 'holding out the infant' criticizes this hypocrisy over social appearances: 'to bend and contrive things so that all would be smooth from the outside, like the way a lazy workman finishes a creel' (p. 135). The minister is forced to retreat by the arrival of Frank and he vainly tries to work on Hamilton in the loanen but to no avail.

The screenplay, however, pointedly switches the initial confrontation from kitchen to churchyard as Sorleyson watches a heavily pregnant Sarah at her mother's grave (fifth draft, scenes 68 and 69) with no words spoken. In the final screen version, the conversation in the novel about the unborn baby's parentage and who Sarah will marry is inserted, finishing with the 'what ails my name?' line. In the screenplay, this is followed by a scene in the Manse House between Sorleyson and his wife harvesting 'tatties' in their kitchen garden plot. He ruefully admits to her: 'Nature is a bad example to simple folk . . . And I am not so sure they are so simple' (scene 70). In the final screen version, this is edited to come *after* scene 71, which shows the Echlin brothers harvesting their potatoes on the lough-side field and Sarah presenting the baby for each to fuss over and admire in turn (see Plate 14). There is a clear indication of Frank's jealousy of Hamilton in a point-of-view shot. Having scene 70 (Sorleyson with his childless wife) followed with scene 72 in the final screen version accentuates Sarah's blissful happiness with her baby, even though he is born out of wedlock.

Plate 14. Who's your daddy? Sarah, baby Andrew and Frank. Photo credit: Simon Mein. Courtesy of Carlton Television.

The screenplay sequence then continues with scene 73 between Sorleyson and Hamilton. Based on exchanges from the novel (pp. 136–137), but with Rudkin's own wicked touch, this becomes one of the most memorable cameo scenes in the film (see Plate 15). The wily Hamilton is the pragmatic farmer busy nursing a new-born lamb which he neatly off-loads onto the awkward minister, the 'good shepherd' trying to cajole one of his 'flock' spiritually. Hamilton sets up Sorleyson by declaring that he will marry Sarah, and the minister brightens momentarily, only for actor Donal McCann to then deliver the punch line with laconic emphasis, 'But she'll not marry me.

Plate 15. The good shepherd and his flock. Sorleyson (Patrick Malahide) and Hamilton (Donal McCann) exchange words. Photo credit: Simon Mein. Courtesy of Carlton Television.

Stubborn huzzy.' The minister's inability to cope with the actual lives of his parishioners outside his narrow moral framework is humorously underlined by his inability to control the lamb in his lap as it shits on his trousers. McCann's twinkle captures Rudkin's direction: 'HAMILTON says nothing. Either he does not notice; or it is the countryman's slow invisible malice at work here. Not even a smile' (fifth draft, p. 67). Hamilton's defence of his position is simple, honest and impregnable ('it's our way and it works'), so much so that Sorleyson resorts to biblical warnings and veiled threats of the social consequences. But Hamilton's quiet fortitude is more than a match for this, and he returns fire with his own biblical allusion: 'crops have been r'ared on stony ground afore'. As if to compound Sorleyson's defeat in the film, his conversation with Sarah in the grain store (II. vii) is the basis for the following scene (scene 74), where again he presses for her to choose a 'father':

SARAH: Marry is it? The child must have a surname? Marry?
SORLEYSON: Sarah, please. . .
SARAH: Marry, and *sanctify the sore*? That's all you want you clergy. To bend and contrive any matter until it's smooth to the eye. All *botched* inside, but outward *smooth to the eye, like lazy work*! (fifth draft, p. 69, my emphasis)

Here Rudkin yokes together powerful images from two separate chapters in the novel (II. v. 135 and vii. 146), modifying 'putting a scab on the sore' with the Latin word 'sanctifying', but adding the blunt vernacular 'botched' (meaning 'clumsily or badly done') and shortening the line to give even greater impact to her reproof. As discussed earlier, the minister's 'carnal curiosity' is aroused by this defiance and he indecently touches her, an act that serves to underline the 'beggarly' (p. 149) nature of all his spiritual arguments. As Sarah comments, 'For all the pious say, there's more nor one recipe for making a house.' The scene is closed by making use of the recurring tidal ford image: O'Sullivan frames Sorleyson retreating to the 'mainland' in long-shot, up to his knees in water, the salty baptism precipitating his departure for a new living in the 'tidy wee town' of Lurgan.

The Lambeg drum shots are crucial elements to some of the most celebrated sequences of the film, but were not in fact envisaged by Rudkin, nor did he really approve of their inclusion in the finished film. To evaluate the merits of their presence, we need to understand the detail of several earlier sequences and track some of the differences between the screenplay drafts, the edited order of the final screen version, and the novel. For instance, the scene between Frank and Hamilton in the haggard at night (scene 76 in the screenplay) is held over in the final version until *after* Sarah's reaction to the rehousing of Bridie Dineen (scenes 77 and 79). In this latter scene Sarah displays a sectarianism that has surfaced before and which has been condemned by the more tolerant Hamilton on more than one occasion. Here, she and Hamilton lock horns over the legal naming of the land and the power that it confers, Sarah retaliating with, 'Oh! That, is it? All about *that*, is it? A *name*?' In the screenplay Sarah is empty-handed during this argument, but in the final screen version she is holding her baby and Rudkin follows this line with one of his own invention in a masterly expression of defiance: 'Well, *my* name is Gomartin – and so is his [gesturing to the baby]. Remember yous that!' (see Plate 16). Momentarily, the minister's authoritarian obsession with 'naming' the child overlaps with the legal patriarchy of Echlin's land-ownership. Whilst Hamilton is quick to seek reconciliation, Frank 'watches awkwardly, aside; unable to intervene' (p. 73), and looks exchanged between himself and Sarah tell us this is a watershed in the relationship. Two 'unmotivated' drumming shots are inserted here in the final screen version, recalling the earlier shots from about five minutes into the film linking an end of kelp-harvesting scene to the pony-cart crossing the landbridge on the Sabbath.

Plate 16. Defiant motherhood. Saskia Reeves as Sarah Gomartin. Photo credit: Simon Mein. Courtesy of Carlton Television.

The Lambeg drum inserts represent a rare divergence in the thinking of Rudkin and his director. They were not Rudkin's idea and arose on location during June 1989 as the marching season built up to its summer climax. Bearing in mind the subject matter he was filming, O'Sullivan felt that the opportunity was too good to miss and organized some sequences to be set up and shot, believing that the drums were 'a great sound motif for the gathering forces . . . this community's war cry'. However, Rudkin has stated plainly:

> I disagreed with Thaddeus about the drums. I felt they were facile as a cultural token, and set up an over-simplified response in the audience . . . Everybody has seen these drums ad nauseam, and has a political attitude to them. (p. 3)

The first appearance of the drummer silhouetted on the skyline at twilight about five minutes into the film corresponds to Bell's one-sentence mention in the novel (II. iv. 127). Whereas the novel goes some way to explaining Old Andrew's (and later Hamilton's) principled non-membership of the Orange Order and his disdain for 'the braggadocio of the belly-drum' (p. 129), early in the film the elder man gruffly mutters 'community' with no little contempt in response to Sarah's asking why he does not like the drums. The interjections provided by the drums at twilight are highly charged, ambiguous audiovisual images. In the latter sequence the long-shot expanse of the mist-covered hills with the drummer in the right foreground and the slowly moving clouds acts as a cue for the brooding atmosphere in the scene between Frank and Hamilton that follows. At one level, these shots stand in for Frank's inner turmoil as he comes to a decision to leave the *ménage*, although he is acutely aware of having placed himself outside of the unforgiving Presbyterian 'community' (note that he echoes his father's contempt). In the scene between the brothers, Rudkin borrows and adapts details and dialogue from Bell (III. v. 245). Hamilton's speech is concentrated in one question ('Frank, are we bad to you?'), and a telling visual gesture of filial tenderness is skilfully retained, but note that it is given to Hamilton to touch Frank's cheek rather than the other way around, as in the original. In the novel, Hamilton mumbles that, 'The three o' us is woven throughother,' but in the final screen version Rudkin has Frank say simply, 'There's no splittin' the two o' ye now,' which is better than the overly poetic lines he is given by Bell.

However, at the level of cultural politics the figure of the Lambeg drummer against the mist-covered hills mitigates a 'romantic' reading of the landscape. As I argued earlier, the County Down countryside of the novel is a husbanded landscape etched with human labour and, in these shots, the geo-cultural proprietorship asserted by the Ulster Protestant majority is literally beaten out as a reminder to the landless Catholics. Considering the dominant tropes of Irish cinema, Martin McLoone observes that:

> The insertion of Orange drums and a devout Presbyterian community into the landscape is a reminder that the industrial workers of Belfast are only part of the Protestant story and the romantic nationalism of Catholic Ireland is only part of the story of the Irish landscape.[80]

And this sense of the partial nature of film representation explains why Rudkin favoured more emphasis being placed on exploring the 'The Field' rather than giving valuable film time to images of drummers. He wanted to explore how scripture examinations, political rallying, socializing and barely-concealed courting could all take place at the event, so that, as Bell observed, 'The fête took on its fuller significance as a communal gathering and a Puritan propitiation to amorous merrymaking' (p. 197). Rudkin felt strongly that, had his scenes been fully realized, 'it would have been a real illumination to many people' (as well as an on-screen celebration for those whose culture it is) and was disappointed that 'a valuable cultural opportunity was lost' (p. 3). That said, Rudkin did acknowledge that the scarf game needed careful story-boarding and that O'Sullivan was working within a very tight shooting schedule.

Aside from these differences, it is clear that the decisive changes from the novel remain: namely, the idea to move the novel's opening wedding to the end of the film (as distinct also from Leitch's earlier version) and to delete the crucial house-building accident (III. 286–288), thus keeping Frank alive. The *ménage à trois* may have run to its own emotional conclusion, but Frank remains part of the household. He ends the film acting *both* as his brother's 'best man' and the bride's absent 'father'. He simultaneously gives away a 'daughter' *and* a lover, to whom he has become a 'father'. Frank's 'supplementarity' as brother, lover and father in this scene makes sense of the novel's configuration of character relationships after Martha moves out of the Echlin farmhouse. As the grouping of a publicity still from the film suggests (Plate 17), if we take Frank and Hamilton as one, then Sarah is at the centre of another 'three-way' relationship with them and Old Andrew. In the novel Sarah's natural father, Charlie Gomartin, was absent in life (he was a nomadic thatcher) and was away in Sligo reportedly dying in mysterious circumstances 'among tinker people' (p. 18). We also know from the novel (but not so clearly from the film) that Margaret Echlin, fed up with the drudgery 'turned her face from her husband and sons' (p. 17) quite suddenly and unexpectedly, but we never learn any more about her. In the film Sarah, critical of her mother's servility and meekness, is prepared to break social convention by remaining in the all-male Echlin household. She becomes an ambivalent figure: substitute 'wife' to Andrew, but also a servant 'mother-lover' to her two sons. This reading resembles the kind of analysis that some have produced for Varda's *Le Bonheur* discussed earlier.

A look at the different openings and endings tried by Rudkin and O'Sullivan offers insights into how the process of adaptation works

Plate 17. Complex, taboo three-way desire at the heart of December Bride. *Photo credit: Simon Mein. Courtesy of Carlton Television.*

as an interpretative and transformative act. In the first draft of the script, Rudkin followed Bell (and Leitch) in opening the film with the marriage ceremony (the son Andrew acting as best man) and the reactions of disgust by locals in the congregation. By the fifth draft, the pre-title imagery is 'wintery', with a long shot of the lough-shore, the silence broken by the wing-beat of a heron taking off suddenly. In the second shot (again an exterior), it is now clearly summer and we witness Martha and Sarah moving out of their cottage. We are told by a title that it is '1900'. This is essentially the order of the final screened version except that in the opening image the heron has been replaced by a wind-blown, bare thorn branch against the lough landscape and the silhouetted figure of a woman to the left of the frame. Rudkin borrowed the leafless 'fairy thorn image' from Leitch's script (this image is itself an invention, and not from the novel), but, whatever its source, the film image is, as Cronin observed of the novel as a whole, 'like some sombre woodcut come wonderfully to life'[81] and a striking index of how the film productively juxtaposes human figures against the natural landscape.[82]

The final moments of the film provide some of the most interesting comparisons between drafts and final cut, and hinge on the absence/presence of Frank. In the first version of the screenplay the ending is a low-key, intimate scene between Hamilton and Sarah just before bedtime:

> He [Hamilton] passes from shot. Merest sound of a bedroom door. We do not move. SARAH's head bows before us; beside her, part side-on, *the empty chair* [Frank's/Old Andrew's?]. Slowly we move around till we stand behind it, looking down on SARAH there. Slowly she wakes; she knows we are here: *she's looking up at us.* SLOW FADE TO BLACK. (fifth draft, p. 124, my emphasis)

The memory of the absent, dead brother (that could also be Old Andrew) and the use of direct gaze at the camera is an attempt at an open, active ending challenging us to consider Sarah's decision to marry or, more broadly, to consider the consequences of decisions she took earlier in her life.

But then, somewhere in the collaborative process of scripting between the first and fifth draft, O'Sullivan persuaded his screenwriter to make a vital change to the story. Rudkin is quite clear that 'to keep Frank alive wasn't my choice, but I understand it, and agree with it . . . Sarah's "choice" between the two brothers has somehow to be still "active" onscreen'.[83] The screenplay for the final scenes ambiguously has a close-up on unidentified hands fitting a ring on a woman's finger, the voice-over of the minister and then 'SARAH flanked by HAMILTON and FRANK at the altar rails'. We may well have guessed that Hamilton is marrying Sarah, but the final screen image of the scene is: 'The trio at the alter, unchanged' (p. 93). Back at the farm, the following scene from the screenplay closes the film as the wedding party are welcomed back 'by the family coming from the house' (Martha, Andrew and Joe Skillen):

> 99. EXT. HAGGARD. DAY.
> (From farther off:) *The whole family of them*: severally making their ways back into the house. Perhaps SARAH even, lifts a bucket in, that stands at the door. Others, ANDREW, JOE, are closing outhouses. FRANK, with one of his crutches, chases a marley-fowl (flap, squawk) from its pecking at a planted bed. *Nothing has been inwardly affected: amid a part-ruled and partly-unruly Nature, a routine resumes.* All are in the house there: some sounds from within there, but the door is now closed. END. (p. 94, my emphasis)

Rudkin's intentions here are clear. He wants us to see the group – including the engaged yet unmarried Joe Skillen, ostracized from his own family – as a 'family' unit that is carrying on, following its own rhythms, despite the social convention of marriage. In the final screened version of the film, we are kept from seeing exactly who Sarah is about to marry in the church by having Frank left of frame and Hamilton right of frame as they sit in the pew waiting for the 'December bride's' arrival. After a close-up of Sarah's face as she walks up the aisle taking in the reactions of the congregation, we cut to a close-up of an unidentified groom's hands putting the wedding ring on Sarah's finger. In the next mid-shot Hamilton is revealed (now *left* of frame) completing this action. The brothers have swapped screen positions and even though she may have married Hamilton, Sarah glances across to Frank.

In a significant reversal of what McLoone has astutely identified as the film's 'signature' treatment of interiors (naturally-lit, claustrophobic, sombre rooms), the next scene is more upbeat, a warm and brightly-lit Echlin household with Joe and Martha dancing to a jig played by Frank on his mouth organ. Unlike the fifth draft, in which we are kept at a distance and shut out, in the final cut we are taken *inside* and are part of the celebration. However, the empty chair image from the first draft is retained (now it must be the memory of Old Andrew) and Martha notices her mother's reflective expression. The closing scene returns us to what happened just before the film's opening shot. Daughter thanks mother for her sacrifice and Sarah's line, 'Our young must live. Things move on,' captures the mood of conciliation based on self-sacrifice and hope for a coming generation. If we follow Rudkin's intended chronology for the setting of the film's action between 1900 and 1918 (and there are indications in the fifth draft that Joe has survived military service), then this new generation of Ulster Protestants faced a rapidly changing and unsettling future; one in which Bell figured significantly from this historical moment on with his arrival in County Down after his father's death. As I have argued, the film's production seventy years after this period provides an important fictional means of remembering that community's history differently, seeing how some within it dared to defy convention, question custom and imagine an alternative if not a perfect future for themselves.

CONCLUSION: OFFERING A FUTURE WITH DIFFERENCE

Accept the fact that a certain number of writers – as of other people – successfully transplant themselves, and that their work is done in two or more contexts.[84]

I have argued that both the novel and the film of *December Bride* are products of creative migrants and that, in trying to understand these works, we need to appreciate the different kinds of contexts with which their artistic energies engaged. I have also argued that adaptation is a productive, transformative interdependent process, and that questions of 'fidelity' to an originary text *per se* present a critical cul-de-sac. To do otherwise is to ignore significant aspects of the conditions in which fiction is written and films are made. In this I have drawn selectively on insights from a burgeoning critical field that examines film adaptations of different kinds of literature. However, following McFarlane, it should be clear that I consider O'Sullivan and Rudkin's film version as a creative commentary[85] on Bell's novel, a remembering of the novel located in its own historical moment at the end of the 1980s. I have also drawn on what is now termed 'diaspora studies', since I agree with the view that, 'much Irish artistic and intellectual activity is impossible to understand without an understanding of migration'.[86] Stressing the discursive, open possibilities of the terms 'regional writing' and 'creative migrancy' helps to release Bell, Rudkin and O'Sullivan from the disabling either/or categories of 'exile' or 'native', of 'Irishness' and 'Britishness'. The mutual exclusivity that these political, cultural and gendered identities have had in the past is precisely what these individuals have sought to interrogate and reconfigure in their creative work. Through an acute sense of an Ulster 'local(e)', the heightened sensibility that migrancy brings to questions of exclusion and plural identity, and through the conscious appropriation of northern European cultural attitudes and cinematic styles, the film of *December Bride* succeeds in reviving and releasing the progressive tendencies implicit in Bell's novel.

In Chapter 1, I outlined the cultural politics of Bell's work and argued for a reading of his novel as regional fiction, a piece of 'necessary provincialism' that smelted its international, Anglo-American literary and theological sources in the crucible of rural Ulster-Scots culture. Bell reminds us that – despite the recent Free Presbyterian proscription of line-dancing in Northern Ireland – creative expression is not wholly anathema to fundamental Protestantism. Indeed, imaginative work by Ulster Protestant writers and artists illuminates the paradoxical coexistence of passion, intellect and faith in productive creativity.[87] In Chapter 2, I outlined the working process of adaptation and analysed the different production contexts that existed for the film of *December Bride*. I argued that Rudkin and O'Sullivan's collaboration produced a more radical text than Bell's novel precisely because they did *not* remain faithful to the text. I argued also that O'Sullivan was conscious of the existing under-representation of Ulster Protestantism in film, and of a dominant tradition in Anglo-American cinematic representations of Ireland more generally, which he actively sought to critique through filming *December Bride*.

In Chapter 3, I explored why and how Rudkin and O'Sullivan tried to locate their film within the aesthetic and production values of a tradition of auteur-centred, European art cinema, consciously imitating and adapting a *mise en scène* from Dreyer and Bergman, and drawing on themes from Varda, Truffaut, and more contemporary figures such as Gabriel Axel (see *Babette's Feast*, 1987). *December Bride* was European in these terms, in respect of significant elements of its creative personnel and its circulation as an art cinema product. But it was materially 'Anglo–Irish' in terms of its funding, production team and cast. In the collaborative pairing of Rudkin and O'Sullivan, Irish roots were firmly sunk in England. While its director and distributor (Colin MacCabe led the BFI vanguard at Cannes) may have accented the film's postnational European-ness, this was not always received as such *in* Europe. As one continental reviewer saw it, with this film, 'The *British* [sic] seem to have started a new style, a kind of regional ethnology and of the past . . . This story of a maid servant who willingly and defiantly chooses to live and be happy with two men is not the rustic *Jules et Jim* one could expect.'[88]

Considered in terms of its funding and production base (London, Film Four Television), *December Bride* forms part of a trend in 1980s film-making that made art-house cinema a distinctive 'British' feature. Yet, shift the frame slightly to contextualize it as an 'Irish' film, with its creative emphasis, location shooting and initial release in Ireland, it represents an alternative, zeitgeist text. In Ireland, *Hush-a-Bye-Baby* (also assisted by Channel Four Television) was circulating at festivals and on release at the same as *December Bride*. While Harkin's film is certainly not art cinema, it nevertheless tackled similar themes, in this case a contemporary story exploring the ramifications of an unmarried teenage girl's pregnancy in Derry's nationalist community. Films like *Hush-a-Bye-Baby* and, later, Gerry Stembridge's *Guiltrip* (1995)[89] formed a small clutch of work that attempted to show a more questioning attitude towards contemporary Ireland that was less tourist-attractive in comparison to the larger-budget productions aimed at the 'quality cross-over' transatlantic Anglo–American market. With *December Bride*, it is noteworthy that a key film to this alternative element in Ireland's contemporary cinema was made by creative migrants based in Britain. In the absence of support within Ireland (the Irish Film Board had been closed down in 1987), and made too soon to take advantage of the EU initiatives to support film that came in the 1990s, *December Bride* emerged out of an economic and cultural between-space. It was conceived and funded outside Ireland, and O'Sullivan and Rudkin were located (but clearly not wholly assimilated) in Britain. *December Bride* has elements of, but does not easily comply with, British or Irish modes of 'heritage' cinema. I would argue that the production represents another instance of Irish creative difference *within* Britain and shows the distinctive possibilities of releasing marginal voices from period film.[90] Considering *December Bride* a decade after its initial release, it is all the more poignant that the majority Ulster Protestant community which marginalizes an internal, disruptive heterodoxy in the film has itself developed a growing realization of being at the uncomfortable edge of a union with two nation-states. Seamus Heaney famously reworked the poetic conceit of Ireland and England as a forced 'act of union'. In *December Bride*, Northern Ireland's current status finds apt expression as a political and cultural *ménage à trois*: awkward, difficult and demanding of trust, but also exploratory, liberating and capable of offering a future with difference.

CREDITS

Alternate titles	La Mariée de l'Hiver
Director	Thaddeus O'Sullivan
Release year	1990
Production year	1989
Production company	Little Bird
	Film Four International
	Central Independent Television
	Ulster TV
	British Screen
Country	Ireland

Cast

Saskia Reeves	Sarah Gomartin
Donal McCann	Hamilton Echlin
Ciaran Hinds	Frank Echlin
Patrick Malahide	Sorleyson
Peter Capaldi	Young Sorleyson
Brenda Bruce	Martha
Michael McKnight	Fergus
Dervla Kirwan	Young Martha
Geoffrey Golden	Echlin
Cathleen Delancy	Agnes
Gabrielle Reidy	Birdie
Frances Lowe	Victoria
Catherine Gibson	Mother Pentland
Julie McDonald	Molly
Roy Heaybeard	Auctioneer
Karl Hayden	Andrew
Miche Doherty	Joe
Peader Lamb	Registrar
George Shane	Orator
Mal Whyte	Shuey
Raymond Barry	Petey
Maurice Hunter	Owen
Maureen Hunter	Egg lady
Michael Wallace	Dineen children
Christopher Wallace	
Catherine O'Hanlon	

Sabrina O'Hanlon	Dineen children *(cont.)*
Michaela O'Hanlon	
George Jeffers	Boatman

Credits

Thaddeus O'Sullivan	Director
James Mitchell	Executive producer
Jonathan Cavendish	Producer
Redmond Morris	Associate producer
Paul Myler	Production accountant
Seamus Byrne	1st assistant director
Christopher Ackland	Dubbing editor
Peter Lindsay	Sound mixer
Mark Huffman	Location manager
Nuala Moiselle	Casting
Susie Figgis	Casting
Tommie Manderson	Make-up supervisor
Joan Carpenter	Chief hairdresser
Gemma Fallon	Production co-ordinator
Alan Galvin	Assistant accountant
Hugh Linehan	Assistant location manager
Konrad Jay	2nd assistant director
Martha O'Neill	3rd assistant director
Margaret Moggan	Trainee assistant director
David Rudkin	Screenplay
Jean Bourne	Script supervisor
Brendan Gunn	Dialogue coach
Andrew Pattman	Script consultant
Jurgen Knieper	Music
Rob Gold	Music consultant
Bruno de Keyser	Director of photography
Dominic Pinto	Focus puller
Brendan Galvin	Clapper loader
Malcom Huse	Camera grip
Seamus Garvey	Camera trainee
Brendan Dempsey	Camera trainee
Simon Mein	Stills photographer
Sean Corcoran	2nd unit photography
Ken Byrne	2nd unit focus puller
Mervyn Moore	Boom operator
Rodney Holland	Editor

Nick Adams	Assistant editor
Mary Finlay	2nd assistant editor
Joe Gilmore	Assistant dubbing editor
Glen Freemantle	Effects editor
Peter Maxwell	Dubbing mixer
Mick Boggis	Assistant dubbing editor
Tim Partridge	Dolby consultant
Consolata Boyle	Costume designer
Richard Pointing	Wardrobe supervisor
Ann O'Halloran	Wardrobe assistant
Karin Cochran	Wardrobe assistant
Magdalen Rubalcava	Design assistant
Vicki Smith	Make-up assistant
Anne Dunne	Hairdresser
Steve Simmonds	Art director
Shirley Henderson	Property buyer
David Balfour	Property master
Cos Egan	Stand-by props
Daragh Lewis	Stand-by props
Nuala McKernan	Dressing props
Peter Gallagher	Dressing props
Pat McKane	Dressing props
Joe McPartland	Prop driver
Gary Walker	Art department driver
Chiz Dube	Producer's assistant
Adrian Smith	Production designer
Joe Kerins	Gaffer
Terry Mitchell	Electrician
Tony Lynch	Electrician
Paddy Higgins	Electrician
Con Dempsey	Rigging gaffer
Maurice Foley	Special effects supervisor
Terry Forrestal	Stunt arranger
Gabe Cronnelly	Stunt doubles
Phil Lonnergan	Stunt doubles
Alfie Joint	Stunt doubles
Tracy Eddon	Stunt doubles
Tommy Basset	Construction manager
Kevin O'Toole	Carpenters
Denis Butler	

James Butler	Carpenters *(cont.)*
Alec Bassett	
Brian Bassett	
Pascal Jones	Riggers
Mick O'Toole	
Bobby Scott	Painters
Alan Scott	
Francis Matthews	Plasterers
James Irwin	
James Lowe	Stagehand
Wilson Knipe	Horsemaster
Rowan McGhie	Ram handler
Running time	90 minutes
Colour code	Colour
Colour system	Technicolor

Notes

1   The stage version was revived by the Lyric Theatre, Belfast, in 1967 and again in 1985 at the Riverside Theatre, Coleraine. The stage script was also adapted for radio with the same title and transmitted by BBC Northern Ireland on 17 October 1963. See Deborah Keys, 'Sam Hanna Bell: A Study of his Contribution Toward the Cultural Development of the Region', unpublished MA dissertation, Queen's University, Belfast, 1982.

2   Seán McMahon, *Sam Hanna Bell: a Biography* (Belfast: Blackstaff Press, 1999), pp. 72, 81–82.

3   The film was first shown on British television on Channel Four at 10 p.m. on 20 October 1992, reaching an audience of 2.571 million, according to BARB. It was shown again in 1996 with sponsorship from Nokia, a wide-screen television manufacturer. The original film was shot in Eastman Colour in Academy (1.66:1) ratio, dimensions associated with a European television standard. It was shown on RTÉ's Network 2 on 24 October 1999 in a later evening slot reaching an audience of 136,000 (representing 20% of the national viewing share).

4   Quoted in McMahon, p. 199.

5   In fact, the publisher Anne Tannahill at Blackstaff Press has indicated that, while the majority of sales are in Ireland (north and south amounting to approximately 70%), a significant readership is found in Britain (15%), the US (10%) and the rest of the world (5%).

6   See the discussion in Deborah Cartmell and Imelda Whelehan, eds. *Adaptations: from Text to Screen, Screen to Text* (London: Routledge, 1999), pp. 3–4.

7   Martin McLoone, *Irish Film: the Emergence of a Contemporary Cinema* (London: BFI, 2000), pp. 122–129.

8   See John Hill, *British Cinema in the 1980s* (Oxford: Oxford University Press, 1999), pp. 73–98, where he discusses the term in this context. For an Irish application to contemporary film, see Ruth Barton, 'From History to Heritage: Some Recent Developments in Irish Cinema', *Irish Review*, No. 21 (Autumn/Winter 1997), pp. 41–56.

9   See Brian McIlroy, 'Challenges and Problems in Contemporary Irish Cinema: the Protestants', *Cineaste*, Vol. 24, Nos. 2–3 (1999), pp. 56–60.

10   References to the novel of *December Bride* are to the Blackstaff Press film tie-in edition (1989), a reprint of the original 1974 paperback edition, with page numbers indicated in the body of the text in

Arabic numerals (e.g. 231) and Part and Chapter number in Roman (e.g. II. vii). References to the different drafts of the screenplay are indicated likewise in the body of the text, citing draft, scene number and/or page number (e.g. fifth draft, scene 79, p. 73).

11   John Wilson Foster, 'The "Dissidence of Dissent": John Hewitt and W. R. Rodgers', in *Across the Roaring Hill: the Protestant Imagination in Modern Ireland*, eds. Gerald Dawe and Edna Longley (Belfast: Blackstaff Press, 1984), p. 141.

12   Edna Longley's essay, 'Progressive Book Men: Left-wing Politics and Ulster Protestant Writers', appeared in 1986 in the *Irish Review*, but references are to a revised version in *The Living Stream: Literature and Revisionism in Ireland* (Newcastle: Bloodaxe Books, 1994), pp. 109–129.

13   John Ellis usefully argues that literary adaptation 'trades upon the memory of the novel, a memory that can derive from actual reading, or, as is more likely with a classic of literature, a generally circulated cultural memory. The adaptation consumes this memory, aiming to efface it with the presence of its own images'. See Ellis, 'The Literary Adaptation: an Introduction', *Screen*, Vol. 23, No. 1 (May/June 1982), p. 3.

14   A. T. Q. Stewart gives a lucid account of 'a Scottish dimension' to the 'Problems of Plantation', in *The Narrow Ground: Patterns of Ulster History* (Belfast: Pretani Press, 1986), pp. 34–41. For a more recent, 'revised' history, see Jonathan Bardon, *A Shorter Illustrated History of Ulster* (Belfast: Blackstaff Press, 1996).

15   Quoted in McMahon, p. 8.

16   Ruth Riddick, *Fortnight*, No. 282 (March 1990), p. 32.

17   See Sophie Hillan King's essay '"A Salute from the Banderol"', in *Writing Ulster*, Vol. 6 (1999), pp. 1–11. Despite John Wilson Foster's inclusion of Bell's work in *Forces and Themes of Ulster Fiction* (1974), Bell has not – until recently – received much sustained consideration. Before his death, Deborah Keys' MA (1982) stands out, as do essays by Longley (1986) and Foster, again in 1988. The *Fortnight* 'obituary' issue of February 1990 included short appraisals of Bell's multifaceted work as broadcaster, editor and fiction writer by Douglas Carson, James Simmons and Patricia Craig.

18   Terence Brown, *The Whole Protestant Community: the Making of a Historical Myth* (Derry: Field Day Pamphlet No. 7, 1985), pp. 17–18.

19   Alvin Jackson, 'Irish Unionist Imagery, 1850–1920' in *Returning to Ourselves*, ed. Eve Patten (Belfast: Lagan Press, 1995), p. 345.

20   S. J. Connolly, ed. *The Oxford Companion to Irish History* (Oxford: Oxford University Press, 1998) has a concise entry on the dissenting tradition in Ireland. He notes that in 1901 there were 443,000 Presbyterians in Ireland, 62,000 Methodists and 60,000 from other Protestant denominations (p. 150).

21   Marianne Elliott, *Watchmen in Sion: the Protestant Idea of Liberty* (Derry: Field Day Pamphlet No. 8, 1985), p. 27.

22   John Hewitt, 'The Bitter Gourd: Some Problems of the Ulster Writer' (originally published in *Lagan*, 1945), in *Ancestral Voices: the Selected Prose of John Hewitt*, ed. Tom Clyde (Belfast: Blackstaff Press, 1987), p. 120.

23   The twelve Republican and Nationalist candidates who won seats in the 1921 election opted to abstain from government, and there was not a Catholic person in any Northern Ireland government until 1969. Essentially, the Stormont parliament governed a one-party state until it was prorogued in 1972 and direct power assumed by Westminster.

24   Patricia Craig, 'The Liberal Imagination in Northern Irish Prose', in *Returning to Ourselves*, ed. Eve Patten (Belfast: Lagan Press, 1995), p. 130.

25   John Hewitt, 'Regionalism: the Last Chance', in *Northman* (1947), reprinted in *Ancestral Voices*, p. 125.

26   K. D. M. Snell, ed. *The Regional Novel in Britain and Ireland, 1800–1990* (Cambridge: Cambridge University Press, 1998), Chapter 1, pp. 1–53, provides an excellent overview of the academic literature in this field, pointing out that advocates of 'regional literature' implicitly support the idea that regional identities and communities may well be more enduring and effective 'units' than nations (p. 53).

27   Douglas Carson, 'A Kist o'Whistles', in 'Radical Ulsters', *Fortnight Supplement*, No. 290 (1990), p. 2.

28   Richard Mills, 'Sam Hanna Bell, 1798 and the Death of Protestant Radicalism', in *New Voices in Irish Criticism*, ed. P. J. Mathews (Dublin: Four Courts Press, 2000), pp. 117, 121.

29   James Simmons, 'A Man Flourishing', in 'Radical Ulsters', *Fortnight Supplement*, No. 290 (1990), p. 3.

30   McMahon, p. 118.

31   McMahon, p. 82.

32   Keys, p. 29.

33   According to Foster, the term 'local naturalism' refers to writers who 'use folk ways in order to recreate a world very different from that

in which most of us live, a rather primitive, ritualistic and insulated world': Foster, *Forces and Themes*, p. 27.

34 See Penny Boumelha's introduction to the new Penguin edition of *The Return of the Native* (London: Penguin, 1999), pp. xx–xxiii.

35 Raymond Williams, *The Country and the City* (London: The Hogarth Press, 1993), p. 197.

36 As quoted in Patricia Craig, 'Out of the Hands of Zealots', *Fortnight*, p. 4. In fact, Craig goes on to say that the novel's 'grim romanticism ... full of rich detail ... [is] a worthwhile achievement but it is rather too static and elemental' to attain the social realism that she claims was Bell's aim.

37 Keys, p. 36.

38 Some features of regional writers identified by K. D. M. Snell seem pertinent to Bell's case, many of whom felt 'displaced by education and mobility from the people and landscape the fiction describes, experiencing a sense of dislodgement or multiple belonging' (Snell, p. 47).

39 John Hewitt, 'Once Alien Here' (1942), in *The Selected John Hewitt*, ed. Alan Warner (Belfast: Blackstaff Press, 1981), p. 20.

40 McMahon, pp. 81–82.

41 Raymond Williams, 'Region and Class in the Novel', in *Writing in Society* (London: Verso, 1983), p. 231.

42 Hardy's *Personal Writings*, quoted in Williams, *The Country and the City*, p. 201.

43 See Anthony Bradley, 'Literature and Culture in the North of Ireland', in *Cultural Contexts and Literary Idioms in Contemporary Irish Literature*, ed. Michael Kenneally (Gerrards Cross, Buckinghamshire: Colin Smythe, 1988), pp. 49–50.

44 Tom Paulin, 'A Necessary Provincialism', in *Two Decades of Irish Writing*, ed. Douglas Dunn (Cheadle, Cheshire: Carcanet Press, 1975), p. 255.

45 In this regard, John Cronin anticipated the first paperback edition in a 1971 essay and also envisaged the educational uses of the novel two generations ahead of the Leaving Certificate examiners in the Republic. See John Cronin, 'Prose', in *Causeway: the Arts in Ulster*, ed. Michael Longley (Belfast and Dublin: Arts Council of Ireland/Gill & Macmillan, 1971), p. 71.

46 John W. Foster, 'Strains in Irish Intellectual Life', in *On Intellectuals and Intellectual Life in Ireland*, ed. Liam O'Dowd (Belfast: IIS/RIA, 1996), p. 92.

47   See Colm Tóibín, ed. *The Penguin Book of Irish Fiction* (London: Penguin, 1999), pp. 618–622, and Patricia Craig, ed., *The Rattle of the North: an Anthology of Ulster Prose* (Belfast: Blackstaff Press, 1992). Craig's choice of excerpt entitled 'New Help at Rathard' is Chapter Two of the novel (pp. 17–22), dealing with the arrival of Sarah and her impact on Old Andrew and the two sons. Sharp-eyed readers will note that she edits the last line out: 'Only Frank, his mind over-cast by his own desires, misinterpreted them' (p. 22).

48   Thaddeus O'Sullivan, tape interview with author, 8 February 2001, at Little Bird office in London. All quotations from O'Sullivan are from this source unless otherwise stated.

49   Letter from David Rudkin to author, 30 January 2001, p. 5. All subsequent quotations from Rudkin refer to this communication (page numbers shown in parenthesis) unless otherwise indicated.

50   Bradley, p. 49.

51   Barton, p. 41.

52   O'Sullivan, quoted in 'A Life Less Ordinary', *Film Ireland*, No. 74 (February/March 2000), p. 20.

53   O'Sullivan, 'Fragments into Pictures' [Interview with Luke Gibbons], *Film Base News*, No. 20 (November/December 1990), p. 10.

54   Set up in 1986, British Screen is a private company (aided by government grant) that 'exists primarily to support new talent and commercially viable productions which might find difficulty in attracting mainstream commercial funding': *BFI Film and Television Handbook 2001* (London: BFI, 2001), p. 268.

55   *Screen International* (28 April 1990), p. 9.

56   *Ordnance Survey of Northern Ireland: Sheet 21* (Strangford Lough, 1: 50,000 scale).

57   Thaddeus O'Sullivan interviewed by Ciaran Carty, the *Irish Times* (c. May 1989), n.p.

58   Kevin Liddy [Review], *Film Base News*, No. 17 (1990), p. 21.

59   Martin McLoone, 'A Landscape Peopled Differently', in *Contemporary Irish Film: from* The Quiet Man *to* Dancing at Lughnasa, ed. James MacKillop (New York: Syracuse University Press, 1999), pp. 48–49.

60   Marcus Crichton, 'The Silver Screen Beckons for Locals as Down Provides Film Backdrop', *Down Recorder*, 28 June 1989, pp. 14–15.

61   See Colin Graham, '"Maybe That's Just Blarney": Irish Culture and the Persistence of Authenticity', in *Ireland and Cultural Theory: the Mechanics of Authenticity*, eds. Colin Graham and Richard Kirkland (Basingstoke: Macmillan, 1999), pp. 7–28.

62 O'Sullivan, quoted in, 'Fragments into Pictures', p. 12. See also Michael Dwyer, 'Clothes Maketh the Movie'[Interview with costume designer Consolata Boyle], the *Irish Times*, Weekend section (27 January 1990), p. 10.

63 Brendan McIlheny, *Empire*, No. 21 (March 1991), p. 38.

64 Thaddeus O'Sullivan, *Time Out*, 6–13 February 1991, p. 27.

65 McLoone, 'A Landscape Peopled Differently', pp. 50–51. At the level of the narrative structure of the film, *December Bride* takes the Hollywood staple of a love-triangle in which two men compete for the love of an available woman, but maintains the three-sided tension until the final scene.

66 Hill, *British Cinema in the 1980s*, p. 65.

67 In this regard, Philip French has pointed out such historical precedents in previous eras: 'much of what was most British about domestic cinema in the 1930s was contributed by foreigners' [*sic*]. See French, 'Is there a European Cinema?', in *Border Crossing: Film in Ireland, Britain and Europe*, eds. John Hill, Martin McLoone and Paul Hainsworth (Belfast: Institute of Irish Studies/BFI, 1994), p. 41.

68 Richard Kearney, *Postnationalist Ireland* (London: Routledge, 1997).

69 Chris Darke, quoted in *The Companion to British and Irish Cinema*, eds. John Caughie and Kevin Rockett (London: Cassell/BFI, 1996), p. 174. See also entries under Forbes et al., in this present book's bibliography.

70 O'Sullivan, quoted in *Thirteenth Durban International Film Festival Programme* (University of Natal, April/May 1991), p. 16.

71 Quoted in Michael Dwyer, *Moving Pictures International* (16 May 1990), p. 24.

72 This is not to say that all viewers will respond positively to this preferred reading, as is demonstrated by the reaction of Robyn Karney (reviewing the film on general release in London in March 1991). Contra to O'Sullivan's best intentions, she read the film as 'predictable': 'so measured in pace, so laden with mood – wild seas, stunning skies, lingering Celtic [*sic*] looks, dark little houses, simple peasants – that it tends to induce a despairing sense of déjà vu'. See *Empire*, No. 21 (March 1991), p. 29. Karney's capacity for misreading the film is not simply one of individual taste but an encultured sense of what an Irish film connotes. This is revealed in signifiers which she strings together in a portmanteau fashion that forces simplistic and inappropriate terms on the screen material, but it does demonstrate the capacity of this discourse to deal with difference.

73 Thaddeus O'Sullivan, interview with the author 8 February 2001. See also Luke Gibbons, 'Framing the Family', in *Encontro da Associao Portuguesa de Estudos Anglo-Americanos* (Vila Real: Actas do XVI Encontro da APEAA, 1996), pp. 155–165.

74 David Bordwell, Janet Staiger and Kristin Thompson, *The Classical Hollywood Cinema: Film Style and Production to 1960* (London: Routledge & Kegan Paul, 1985), p. 5.

75 This is discussed by Keith Hopper in '"Cat-Calls from the Cheap Seats": the Third Meaning of Neil Jordan's *Michael Collins*', *Irish Review*, No. 27 (Autumn/Winter 1997), pp. 25–26.

76 O'Sullivan also discussed the possibility of a further subtextual sexual attraction between Sarah and Old Andrew that is hinted at but not developed in the film. See O'Sullivan, 'Fragments in Pictures', p. 11. In the novel, Sarah's servant-girl attraction to Andrew is given a pragmatic economic basis. (see I.ii.22).

77 *Le Bonheur* is currently available on video (NTSC format) in French with English subtitles in a restored and digitally remastered version (Chicago, Home Vision Cinema, 1997).

78 For details, see Ginette Vincendeau's entry on Varda in *The Women's Companion to International Film*, ed. Anette Kuhn with Susannah Radstone (London: Virago, 1990), pp. 411–412.

79 Alison Smith's reading of the film in *Agnès Varda* (Manchester: Manchester University Press, 1998), pp. 43–45, makes this point. See also Sandy Flitterman-Lewis's important chapter, 'Agnès Varda and the Woman Seen', in *To Desire Differently: Feminism and the French Cinema* (Urbana and Chicago: University of Illinois Press, 1990), pp. 215–247. My thanks to Fidelma Farley for pointing out this reference to me.

80 McLoone, *Irish Film*, p. 209.

81 Cronin, p. 71. Keith Hopper has pointed out that the literary source for this image might well be Samuel Ferguson's poem 'The Fairy Thorn' (1834).

82 Martin McLoone, 'A Landscape Peopled Differently', p. 40.

83 Rudkin, letter to author 30 January 2001, p. 3.

84 Sam Hanna Bell, ed., *The Arts in Ulster* (London: Harrap, 1951), p. 117.

85 Brian McFarlane, *Novel to Film: an Introduction to the Theory of Adaptation* (Oxford: Clarendon Press, 1996), pp. 21–22.

86 Patrick O'Sullivan, *The Creative Migrant: the Irish World Wide*, Vol. 3 (Leicester: Leicester University Press, 1997), p. 2.

87   See Barry Sloan's recent book, *Heirs to Adamnation: Writers and Protestantism in the North of Ireland* (Dublin: Irish Academic Press, 2001).

88   Phillipe Garnier, translated from, 'Une Austère Mariée en Ulster', *Libération* (19–20 May 1990), p. 33.

89   This film was European in another sense that became increasingly more prevalent in 1990s Irish film-making in that it was funded through a complicated set of co-production arrangements with European film and television backers and EU support mechanisms. See Angus Finney's case study in *The State of European Cinema* (London: Cassell, 1996), pp. 230–239.

90   Andrew Higson, 'The Heritage Film and British Cinema', in *Dissolving Views: Key Writings on British Cinema*, ed. Andrew Higson (London: Cassell, 1996), p. 244.

Bibliography

Note: press reviews [Review], interviews [Interview] and articles related to *December Bride* are drawn from cuttings collections held by Little Bird and the British Film Institute in London, the Film Institute of Ireland in Dublin and the Central Library, Belfast. It has not been possible to record complete bibliographical details in all cases, since the original cuttings were not fully annotated or attributed to a named author.

Anon. 'Movie-Makers at the Ards Peninsular'. *Newtownards Chronicle* (15 June 1989): 3.

Anon. 'Saskia – A Busy "Bride"'. *Sunday Independent* (25 February 1990): n.p.

Anon. 'Saskia's Stage Set'. *The Business of Film at Cannes*, No. 9 (18 May 1990): 14.

Axel, Gabriel. *Babette's Feast*. Denmark: 1987.

Bardon, Jonathan. *A Shorter Illustrated History of Ulster*. Belfast: Blackstaff Press, 1996.

Baron, Jeanine. [Review] *La Croix* (20 May 1990): n.p.

Barton, Ruth. 'From History to Heritage: Some Recent Developments in Irish Cinema'. *Irish Review*, No. 21 (1997): 41–56.

Baveystock, Freddie. 'Local Scandal: Film Four Delves into Moral and Political Controversy'. *Screen at Cannes* (17 May 1990): n.p.

Bell, Sam Hanna. *December Bride*. Belfast: Blackstaff Press, 1990.

——. *Erin's Orange Lily and Summer Loanen & Other Stories*. Belfast: Blackstaff Press, 1996.

——. 'Ulster Prose', in *The Arts in Ulster: a Symposium*, eds. Sam Hanna Bell, Nesca Robb and John Hewitt. London: Harrap, 1951. 99–127.

Bergman, Ingmar. *Through a Glass Darkly*. Sweden: 1961.

Bordwell, David, Janet Staiger and Kristin Thompson. *The Classical Hollywood Cinema: Film Style and Production to 1960*. London: Routledge & Kegan Paul, 1985.

Bradley, Anthony. 'Literature and Culture in the North of Ireland', in *Cultural Contexts and Literary Idioms in Contemporary Irish Literature*, ed. Michael Kenneally. Gerrards Cross, Buckinghamshire: Colin Smythe, 1988. 36–72.

Brown, Geoff. [Review] *The Times* (7 February 1991): 17.

Brown, Terence. *The Whole Protestant Community: the Making of a Historical Myth*. Derry: Field Day Pamphlet No. 7, 1985.

Byrge, Duane. [Review] *Hollywood Reporter* (15 January 1991): 11, 178.

Campbell, Flann. *The Dissenting Voice: Protestant Democracy in Ulster from Plantation to Partition*. Belfast: Blackstaff Press, 1991.

Carr, Jay. 'More of Ireland's Cinematic Strength'. *Boston Globe* (16 April 1993): 85.

Carson, Douglas. 'A Kist o' Whistles'. *Fortnight Supplement*, No. 290 (1990): 2.

——. 'Sam Hanna Bell 1909–1990'. *Honest Ulsterman*, No. 89 (Summer 1990): 43–52.

Cartmell, Deborah, and Imelda Whelehan. Eds. *Adaptations: from Text to Screen, Screen to Text*. London: Routledge, 1999.

Carty, Ciaran. 'The Art of Making Dublin a Euro City of Culture on the Cheap'. *Sunday Tribune* (30 December 1990): 28.

Carty, Ciaran. [Interview with O'Sullivan] *Irish Times*, c. February 1990, n.p.

Cleary, Paul. [Review] *Hot Press*, (n.d.): 24.

Connolly, S. J. Ed. *The Oxford Companion to Irish History*. Oxford: Oxford University Press, 1998.

Coogan, Anna. 'The Infernal Triangle'. *Evening Herald* (21 November 1900): 31.

Craig, Patricia. 'The Liberal Imagination in Northern Irish Prose', in *Returning to Ourselves*, ed. Eve Patten. Belfast: Lagan Press, 1995. 130–144.

——. 'Out of the Hands of Zealots'. *Fortnight Suplement*, No. 290 (1990): 4.

——. Ed. *The Rattle of the North: an Anthology of Ulster Prose*. Belfast: Blackstaff Press, 1992.

Caughie, John, and Kevin Rockett. *The Companion to British and Irish Cinema*. London: Cassell/BFI, 1996.

Crichton, Marcus. 'The Silver Screen Beckons for Locals as Down Provides Film Backdrop'. *Down Recorder* (28 June 1989): 14–15.

Cronin, John. 'Prose', in *Causeway: the Arts in Ulster*, ed. Michael Longley. Belfast and Dublin: Arts Council of Ireland/Gill & Macmillan, 1971. 71–83.

Cunningham, Francine. [Interview with Saskia Reeves] 'Pretending to be Someone Else – Truthfully'. *Irish Times* (10 December 1990): 14.

——. 'Tender Triad Caught in a Small World'. *Irish Times* (23 November 1990): 14.

Davenport, Hugo. [Review] *Daily Telegraph* (6 February 1991): 15.

Dawe, Gerald, and Edna Longley. Eds. *Across the Roaring Hill: the Protestant Imagination in Modern Ireland*. Belfast: Blackstaff Press, 1984.

Daws. [Review] *Variety: Daily Screening Guide* (18 May 1990): 10.

December Bride/La Mariée de L'Hiver. Directors' Fortnight Programme (May 1990).

Dreyer, Carl. *Day of Wrath* (Denmark: Palladium Film, 1943).

———. *Ordet* (Denmark: Palladium Film, 1954).

Drummond, Philip, et al. Eds. *National Identity and European Cinema*. London: BFI, 1983.

Dwyer, Michael. 'Clothes Maketh the Movie'. *Irish Times* (27 January 1990): 10.

———. 'Directors' Fortnight: *December Bride*'. *Moving Pictures International* (16 May 1990): 24.

Elliott, Marianne. *Watchmen in Sion: the Protestant Idea of Liberty*. Derry: Field Day Pamphlet No. 8 (1985).

Ellis, John. 'The Literary Adaptation: an Introduction'. *Screen*, Vol. 23, No. 1 (May/June 1982): 3–5.

Everett, Wendy. Ed. *European Identity in Cinema*. Exeter: Intellect Books, 1996.

Finney, Angus. *The State of European Cinema: a New Dose of Reality*. London: Cassell, 1996.

Fitzgerald, Charles. 'Author Dies in Hospital'. *Ulster Newsletter* (12 February 1990): 2.

Flitterman-Lewis, Sandy. *To Desire Differently: Feminism and the French Cinema*. Urbana and Chicago: University of Illinois Press, 1990.

Floyd, Nigel. 'On Thaddeus O'Sullivan'. *Time Out* (6–13 February 1991): 27.

Forbes, Jill, et al. *European Cinema: an Introduction*. Houndmills, Basingstoke: Palgrave, 2000.

Foster, John Wilson, *Colonial Consequences: Essays in Irish Literature and Culture*. Dublin: Lilliput Press, 1991.

———. *Forces and Themes in Ulster Fiction*. Dublin: Gill & Macmillan, 1974.

———. 'Strains in Irish Intellectual Life', in *On Intellectuals and Intellectual Life in Ireland*, ed. Liam O'Dowd. Belfast: Institute for Irish Studies/Royal Irish Academy, 1996. 71–97.

Garnier, Phillipe. 'Une Austere Mariée en Ulster'. *Libération* (19–20 May 1990): 33.

Gibbons, Luke. [Interview with Thaddeus O'Sullivan] 'Fragments into Pictures'. *Film Base News*, No. 20 (November/December 1990): 8–12.

———. 'Framing the Family', in *Encontra de Associao Portguesa de Estudos Anglo-Americanos*. Vila Real: Actas do Encontro da APEAA, 1996: 155–165.

Giddings, Robert, Keith Selby, and Chris Wensley. *Screening the Novel: the Theory and Practice of Literary Dramatization*. London: Macmillan, 1990.

Hardy, Thomas. *The Return of the Native*. London: Penguin, 1999.

Hewitt, John. *Ancestral Voices: the Selected Prose of John Hewitt*, ed. Tom Clyde. Belfast: Blackstaff Press, 1987.

——. *The Selected John Hewitt*, ed. Alan Warner. Belfast: Blackstaff Press, 1981.

Higson, Andrew. *Dissolving Views: Key Writings on British Cinema*. London: Cassell, 1996.

Hill, John. *British Cinema in the 1980s*. Oxford: Oxford University Press, 1999.

Hill, John, Martin McLoone and Paul Hainsworth. Eds. *Border Crossing: Film in Ireland, Britain and Europe*. Belfast: Institute of Irish Studies/BFI, 1994.

Hopper, Keith. '"Cat-Calls from the Cheap Seats": the Third Meaning of Neil Jordan's *Michael Collins*'. *Irish Review*, No. 27 (Autumn/Winter, 1997): 1–28.

Horning, Glynis. [Review] 'Thirteenth Durban International Film Festival'. *The Natal Mercury* (17 April 1991): n.p.

Jackson, Alvin. 'Irish Unionist Imagery, 1850–1920', in *Returning to Ourselves*, ed. Eve Patten. Belfast: Lagan Press, 1995: 344–359.

Johnston Alexander. [Review] 'Durban International Film Festival'. Untitled press cutting, Durban, South Africa (21 April 1991): 16.

Kearney, Richard. *Postnationalist Ireland: Politics, Culture, Philosophy*. London: Routledge, 1997.

Kermode, Mark. [Review], *Monthly Film Bulletin*, Vol. 58, No. 685 (1991): 43–44.

Keys, Deborah. 'Sam Hanna Bell: a Study of his Contribution Toward the Cultural Development of the Region'. Unpublished MA dissertation, Queen's University, Belfast, 1982.

King, Sophie Hillan. '"A Salute from the Banderol": Sam Hanna Bell's Contribution to Ulster's Cultural Life'. *Writing Ulster*, No. 6 (1999): 1–11.

La Croisette, H. 'Thad's Tough Time' *The Business of Film at Cannes*, No. 5 (14 May 1990): 30.

Leitch, Maurice. *December Bride: a Screenplay*. 97pp. bound typescript, n.d.

Licht, Daniel. 'Le Coup de Jeune de Festival D'Annonay'. *Libération* (13 February 1991): 5.

Liddy, Kevin. [Review] *Film Base News*, No. 17 (1990): 21–22.

Longley, Edna. *The Living Stream: Literature and Revisionism in Ireland*. Newcastle: Bloodaxe Books, 1994.

Macafee, C. I. Ed. *Concise Ulster Dictionary*. Oxford: Oxford University Press, 1996.

Malcolm, Derek. [Review] *The Guardian* (7 February 1991): 29.

McCarthy, Gerry. [Review] *In Dublin* (22 November–December 1990): 101–102.

McFarlane, Brian. *Novel to Film: an Introduction to the Theory of Adaptation*. Oxford: Clarendon Press, 1996.

McIlroy, Brian. 'Challenges and Problems in Contemporary Irish Cinema: the Protestants'. *Cineaste*, Vol. 24, Nos. 2–3 (1999): 56–60.

——. *Shooting to Kill: Filmmaking and the 'Troubles' in Northern Ireland*. Trowbridge: Flicks Books, 1998.

McLoone, Martin. 'A Landscape Peopled Differently', in *Contemporary Irish Film: from* The Quiet Man *to* Dancing at Lughnasa. ed. James MacKillop. New York: Syracuse University Press, 1999: 40–53.

McLoone, Martin. 'Urban Ireland's Rural Landscape'. in *Irish Film: the Emergence of a Contemporary Cinema*. London: BFI, 2000, 201–212.

McMahon, Seán. *Sam Hanna Bell: a Biography*. Belfast: Blackstaff Press, 1999.

Mills, Richard. 'Sam Hanna Bell, 1798 and the Death of Protestant Radicalism', *New Voices in Irish Criticism*, ed. P. J. Mathews. Dublin: Four Courts Press, 2000. 116–122.

O'Neill, Nicholas. 'Star of the County Down'. *Sunday Press* (25 February 1990): n.p.

O'Sullivan, Patrick. *The Creative Migrant: the Irish World Wide*, Vol. 3. Leicester: Leicester University Press, 1994.

O'Sullivan, Thaddeus. *December Bride*. Britain/Ireland: Little Bird/ Connoisseur, 1992.

——. 'December Bride', in *Cannes Film Festival Programme: Directors' Fortnight*. [Programme note, in French with English translation].

Patten, Eve. Ed. *Returning to Ourselves: Second Volume of Papers from the John Hewitt International Summer School*. Belfast: Lagan Press, 1995.

Paulin, Tom. 'A Necessary Provincialism', *Two Decades of Irish Writing*, ed. Douglas Dunn. Cheadle, Cheshire: Carcanet Press, 1975. 242–256.

Perneud, Paschal. *Positif*, No. 353/354 (July/August 1990): 86.

Petrie, Duncan. Ed. *Screening Europe*. London: BFI, 1992.

Pettitt, Lance. *Screening Ireland: Film and Television Representation*. Manchester: Manchester University Press, 2000.

Riddick, Ruth. [reporting on Dublin Film Festival] *Fortnight*, No. 282 (March 1990): 32.

Rudkin, David. *December Bride: First Draft Screenplay*. 124pp unbound typescript, June 1988.

——. *December Bride: Fifth Draft Screenplay*. 94pp bound typescript, July 1988.

——. *December Bride: Eighth Draft Revisions*. 15pp unbound handwritten, n.d.

Shanahan, Kate. [Interview] 'Thaddeus – Projecting Emotion'. *Irish Press* (9 January 1991): 20–21.

Sheehy, Ted. [Caption review] *In Dublin* (22 November–5 December 1990): 78–79.

Simmons, James. 'A Man Flourishing'. *Fortnight Supplement*, No. 290 (1990): 3.

Sinyard, Neil. *Filming Literature: the Art of Screen Adaptation*. London: Croom Helm, 1986.

Sloan, Barry. *Heirs to Adamnation: Writers and Protestantism in the North of Ireland*. Dublin: Irish Academic Press, 2001.

Smith, Alison. *Agnès Varda*. Manchester: Manchester University Press, 1998.

Smith, Anne-Marie. 'Reluctant Winner's December Pride'. *Sunday Tribune* (c. December 1990): n.p.

Smyth, Damien. Ed. 'Radical Ulsters'. *Fortnight* Special Supplement, No. 290 (January 1991): 1–11.

Snell, K. D. M. Ed. *The Regional Novel in Britain and Ireland, 1800–1990*. Cambridge: Cambridge University Press, 1998.

Sorlin, Pierre. *European Cinemas, European Societies: 1939–1990*. London: Routledge, 1991.

Stewart, A. T. Q. *The Narrow Ground: Patterns of Ulster History*. Belfast: Pretani Press, 1986.

Stidolph, Anthony. [Review] *Natal Witness* [South Africa] (7 May 1991): n.p.

Tóibín, Colm. Ed. *The Penguin Book of Irish Fiction*. London: Penguin, 1999.

V.S. [Review] 'La Mariée de l'Hiver'. *Le Film Français* Supplement, No. 2296 (6 Mai 1990): n.p.

Wallace, Martin. '"Sound Ulsterman" Profile: Sam Hanna Bell'. *Belfast Telegraph* (5 January 1962): n.p.

Williams, Raymond. *The Country and the City*. London: The Hogarth Press, 1993. 197–214.

——. 'Region and Class in the Novel', in *Writing in Society*. London: Verso, 1983. 229–238.

Woodworth, Paddy. 'Festival Showed Dublin's Appetite for Arts'. *Irish Times* (5 March 1990): n.p.